UNCONVENTIONAL WOMEN

MARGARET HESS

While this book is designed for the reader's personal enjoyment and profit, it is also intended for group study. A Leader's Guide with Victor Multiuse Transparency Masters is available from your local bookstore or from the publisher.

VICTOR BOOKS

a division of SP Publications, Inc.
WHEATON, ILLINOIS 60187

Offices also in Fullerton, California • Whitby, Ontario, Canada • Amersham-on-the-Hill, Bucks, England

Second printing, 1982

Recommended Dewey Decimal Classification: 219
  Suggested Subject Heading: WOMEN IN THE BIBLE

Library of Congress Catalog Card Number: 81-50683
ISBN:0-88207-340-0

VICTOR BOOKS
A division of SP Publications, Inc.
P.O. Box 1825 ● Wheaton, Illinois 60187

CONTENTS

To my husband, Bart,
for inspiration, encouragement, and criticism

———

To Marilynn Adams,
Eileen Prestel, and Nancy Edgar
for assistance in typing

PREFACE

Unconventional women accept themselves as God made them, pursuing their own goals as God directs them. We find them in today's world, we find them in the Bible. This book brings the Bible alongside life today and shows us how to cope with everyday situations in unconventional ways. We learn how to free ourselves creatively from accepted patterns that limit living.

This book examines Bible characters representative of women in today's world: Deborah, who led her nation. The ideal woman of Proverbs, who functioned as wife, mother, and businesswoman. The woman at the well, who lived with a man who was not her husband. The five daughters of Zelophehad, who weren't afraid to ask. Eve, who faced the opportunities and temptations of the woman at home. The widow of Zarephath, who learned to cope as a single parent.

We examine Lydia, the businesswoman who made her impact for Christ as a single. Miriam, another single, who learned about jealousy the hard way. Leah, who lived with relationships as complicated as those of the modern reconstituted family. The maid in Naaman's household, who showed what a blue-collar worker can do. Jezebel, who teaches us by reverse example.

These Bible women, along with the contemporary women in this book, teach us how to meet the challenges and tests of living for Christ today.

1
How to
Be a Leader

Golda Meir grew up in Milwaukee, Wisconsin. When her children were teenagers, she saw a need for people who would help to build the nation of Israel. So she emigrated from the wealth and comfort of America to cast her lot with a struggling and threatened country. Eventually she became prime minister, leading Israel through terrible adversity and to a great victory.

Golda Meir became a "mother in Israel" to an entire nation.

In the early part of our century, a mass of newcomers from Europe were settling on the west side of Chicago. Arriving straight from the Jewish ghettos of Poland, Russia, and Lithuania, they experienced a lot of trouble in getting jobs, learning English, and finding housing.

Anna Heistad saw a need and an opportunity. She wanted to teach these people about Jesus while helping them adjust to American life. The Methodist Church backed her in the project of establishing a neighborhood house. As she taught them English, she also taught them the Bible. Many of the people she ministered to became fulfilled Jews, accepting Jesus as their Messiah.

Anna Heistad, a Gentile, became a "mother in Israel" to a whole generation of Jews in the Pulaski-26th Street area of Chicago's west side.

At our church in Detroit, we desperately needed someone to take charge of the nurseries while mothers attended Bible class.

Paid workers were keeping the children safe. But we had prayed for someone to take charge—a woman with a vision for teaching toddlers and preschoolers of the Christian faith.

The class chairman approached three or four women, but all had good reasons for not taking the job. Then she called Barbara.

"I'd love to," said Barbara. "That's just exactly what I'd like to do. I've been praying for something to do for the Lord, a job that I was qualified for. It seemed there just wasn't anything I'd be good at—till you called. Thank you for asking me."

Barbara became a "mother in Israel" to workers and children alike.

Deborah

Who was the original "mother in Israel?" Deborah. How did she get to be first in her nation? By having so much to offer that all Israel came to her. Even the leading general insisted on being second to her. Deborah saw a need and responded to it.

What was the need? "Then the sons of Israel again did evil in the sight of the Lord, after Ehud died. And the Lord sold them into the hand of Jabin king of Canaan, who reigned in Hazor" (Jud. 4:1-2).

Over and over the Israelites turned away from God who had done so much for them. They served the Baals and the Astartes with their awful temple prostitution and child sacrifice. Each time God became angry that His own children should behave so unworthily. As discipline, He "sold them into the hands of their enemies," and the Israelites suffered the miseries of defeat. When at last they cried out to God, he raised up judges to deliver them. The general pattern is described in Judges 2:11-19.

Those judges came to the fore by sheer force of superior qualifications. Deborah was the only woman in the Bible placed at the height of political power by the common consent of the people. She had no royal lineage, and was the wife of an obscure man.

As Deborah was growing up, the land was ruled by Jabin, a Canaanite from the city of Hazor. The ruins of Hazor have been identified a little to the southwest of the now-drained Lake Huleh in Galilee.

Little Deborah, living the hard life of a girl in that society, saw the afflictions God's people were suffering. Whatever meager education was available for boys in that day was more than was provided for girls. For their days were filled with learning household tasks, carrying water morning and evening, and watching a few sheep on the hillside. Deborah's name means "bee." She was no doubt a busy little girl, assuming responsibilities early. But that did not make her a likely candidate for inspiring a whole nation.

Yet somehow Deborah gained the training she needed. Perhaps she had a father who taught her the stories and songs of Israel. Even amid universal decay, God does not leave His people without a witness. Always a few refuse to bow the knee to Baal. Perhaps Deborah had brothers who were taught and who relayed their learning to her. Perhaps she had a mother with a vision for her, a mother who believed that her daughters could develop their minds and hearts for God.

My mother grew up on a farm in Iowa, as one of four girls. Neither of her parents had more than a few years of schooling. Yet they both had a vision for their daughters, and offered each an education. My mother graduated from college—a rare feat in those days. She taught school, married a minister, and served the church all her life.

My husband's mother grew up in a poor home in Worcester, Massachusetts. Her stepmother worked hard, but had no vision for the girl's development. Jessie had to drop out of school after the tenth grade to work. She did secretarial work, married a minister, studied all her life, and became an outstanding Bible teacher.

Long before the days of women's lib, individual women, with or without parental encouragement, found ways to develop their talents. Somehow Deborah developed qualities that made all Israel seek her out for counsel, inspiration, advice, and judgment.

Jabin's Army

King Jabin had appointed Sisera as commander of his army. "And the sons of Israel cried to the Lord; for he had 900 iron chariots, and he oppressed the sons of Israel severely for 20 years" (Jud. 4:3).

Those 900 chariots of iron were the atomic weapons of that day. The Israelites clung to the hillsides, leaving the more fertile valleys in total control of the Canaanites. Because the nation lay in abject terror of the mighty Sisera with his chariots, the Israelites endured all kinds of indignities. Deborah described these in some detail in her song.

"The highways were deserted, and travelers went by round-about ways. The peasantry ceased, they ceased in Israel. . . . New gods were chosen; then war was in the gates. Not a shield or a spear was seen among 40,000 in Israel" (Jud. 5:6-8).

They suffered under such heavy taxation and petty attack that agriculture and village life of those working the land practically ceased.

No more caravans moved on the great highroad that passed through the valley of Jezreel, connecting Egypt with the rich Euphrates valley to the east. Travelers kept to the byways, fearful of the powerful Jabin.

Israel misinterpreted God's chastening. Thinking He had lost His power to protect them, they tried other gods. Then God allowed war to approach to the very gates of their cities. Among the 40,000 in Israel, no one possessed the courage to stand with a weapon against the tyrant.

For 20 years Jabin oppressed Israel. No doubt he thought himself a great man, as lord and ruler over Israel. No doubt he counted Israel as part of his riches.

The Prophetess

Somehow Israel struggled along, trying to cope with day-to-day problems. "Now Deborah, a prophetess, the wife of Lappidoth, was judging Israel at that time. And she used to sit under the palm tree of Deborah between Ramah and Bethel in the hill country of Ephraim: and the sons of Israel came up to her for judgment" (Jud. 4:4-5).

If she had followed the standard pattern for young Israelite girls, Deborah would have been married in her early teens to a man selected by her parents. We hear nothing more about her husband, Lappidoth, or Deborah's relationship to him. Lappidoth may have been very busy as a farmer earning a living for both of them. That part of the country, north of Jerusalem on the central ridge of mountains, is now devoted largely to vineyards and olive orchards. He may have been supportive of her efforts to help the nation, and proud that many sought her counsel.

Said a woman executive in the automotive industry, "My husband is secure enough in his masculinity that he doesn't feel threatened by my success." Many a successful person has said, "I couldn't possibly have done it without my spouse's complete cooperation."

Deborah probably lived in a rude hut with walls built of the local limestone, and with a flat roof thatched from clay and branches. She performed the usual duties of a wife—weaving, grinding grain, baking the flat loaves of bread over a fire.

But Deborah was comparatively freer than other women, for she had no children. From the time a woman bore a son, she was identified as his mother. So any children of Deborah would certainly have been mentioned. Bearing children was considered the supreme honor for any Israelite woman.

We don't know if Deborah sorrowed over this lack. But we do know that she developed marvelous qualities of motherhood and made those qualities available to any who sought her out.

A modern woman, Nancy, expresses what may have been Deborah's feelings. Nancy—well educated, supported by her husband, and without children—makes a career of volunteer work. She said, "I think we would have made good parents. But the Lord didn't give us any children. When you're living really close to the Lord, as Jerry and I try to do, you just leave such things with Him. I've kept busy. There has always been something that I considered important for me to do. Jerry likes to have me spend my time in Christian work. Not having children hasn't affected our marriage; we're both happy serving the Lord."

Nancy keeps seeing needs. She's been a second mother to various young people. She has also used her gifts of administration to minister to hundreds.

Deborah saw the need of Israel, and suffered with those afflicted. She also suffered for the honor of Jehovah. We don't detect in her any personal ambition. She didn't set out to be first in the nation. God put her there—"the Lord raised up judges" (Jud. 2:16).

Why a Woman?

Why would God call a woman to summon a whole nation to resistance? Perhaps He wanted to remind them that it was " 'not by might nor by power, but by My Spirit' " that victory could be attained (Zech. 4:6).

Deborah's first concern was for her own relationship to God Almighty. She knew the secret of strength that is "perfected in weakness" (2 Cor. 12:9). God's strength in her made strong men stronger, and weak men able to carry on.

The word spread. One by one people came to her for counsel, for encouragement, for advice, for fair judgment. Gradually she emerged as the highest court of all Israel. (See Deut. 17:8-9.) The nation was supposed to be a theocracy, with all looking to God as the Head. Deborah did look to God, and all Israel knew it. No one set her up in a lavish palace. She simply sat under a palm tree outside her home, on the road that winds through the hills between Bethel and Ramah. There she held unofficial court.

As Deborah talked with all those people, she heard their stories of suffering at the hands of Jabin's archers. She listened to descriptions of the chariots as they maneuvered and struck terror to all hearts.

Deborah felt pressed to do something, to act for God. "Now she sent and summoned Barak the son of Abinoam" (Jud. 4:6). Deborah summoned a general from faraway Kedesh-naphtali, up north in the region of Jabin's headquarters. Barak apparently didn't quibble over answering the summons of a woman. Nor did anybody else worry about whether God's message was coming through a woman or a man.

Says G. Campbell Morgan, the great Bible expositor,
In the light of subsequent Jewish prejudice against women as leaders, the story of Deborah is full of interest, as it reveals

the fact that there never was any such prejudice in the mind of God. . . . Deborah was a prophetess in the full sense of that word. . . . She was the inspired mouthpiece of the Word of God to her people. . . . The one great message of the story seems to be that it warns us to take heed that we do not imagine ourselves to be wiser than God. When He calls and equips a woman to high service, let us beware lest we dishonor Him by refusing to recognize her or cooperate with her *(Searchlights from the Word).*

An Inspiring Woman

Deborah said to Barak, "Behold, the Lord, the God of Israel, has commanded, 'Go and march to Mount Tabor, and take with you 10,000 men from the sons of Naphtali and from the sons of Zebulun. And I will draw out to you Sisera, the commander of Jabin's army, with his chariots and his many troops . . . and I will give him into your hand'" (Jud. 4:6-7).

Deborah didn't assume the generalship herself. Other judges had led the troops into battle and God had given them mighty victories. Deborah showed her selflessness in summoning a man for the honor of leadership. She made herself available for God's purposes, but God didn't ask her to fight. He called her to inspire those who would fight. Many women today feel the greatest thing they have done is to inspire men to great accomplishments.

Deborah's message to Barak: he was simply to obey God and go into battle. God would provide the victory. But Barak trembled in dread. As a military man he knew the incongruity of matching Israel's pitiful force against mighty chariots of iron.

Yet Barak sensed the power of God behind Deborah's words. He felt he could manage the military end of things if Deborah would go along to keep up his courage and inspire the troops. He knew they would need superhuman trust and superhuman action.

"Then Barak said to her, 'If you will go with me, then I will go; but if you will not go with me, I will not go'" (Jud. 4:8).

Barak showed bravery in promising to undertake the impossible task. But we detect a hint of disappointment, even annoyance in Deborah as she replied, "'I will surely go with you; nevertheless, the honor shall not be yours on the journey that you are about to take, for the Lord will sell Sisera into the hands of a woman.' Then Deborah arose and went with Barak to Kedesh" (Jud. 4:9).

Again, Deborah didn't push herself forward. She only responded to a need. The leader of the army required her presence. She gave up her own comforts at home to go. She knew in her heart that what he seemed to be asking her to do—offer courage and inspiration—she could do. So she did it.

A missionary couple was enormously successful in establishing pioneer mission work. The man appeared the more gifted and able of the two. Yet when his wife died, his courage collapsed. She was the one who all along had inspired him to impossible tasks. They had supplemented each other's abilities to accomplish great things for God.

Deborah was content to be part of a team. She didn't seek the limelight for herself, but would gladly give it to Barak. And he wasn't worrying about which sex the ultimate gift of leadership had fallen on. He only knew that without her he couldn't accomplish the task.

We're all incomplete in ourselves. To function effectively as parts of the body of Christ, we need each other. As we die to self and set our own egos aside, God can show us how we fit together to accomplish His work in the world.

Strangely enough, Barak is named among the heroes of faith, but Deborah is not (Heb. 11:32). I don't believe it would have mattered to Deborah.

Deborah the Strategist

"And Barak called Zebulun and Naphtali together to Kedesh, and 10,000 men went up with him; Deborah also went up with him" (Jud. 4:10).

Deborah wasn't one of those armchair strategists who say, "You all go out and risk your lives. I'll stay well behind the lines and protect my own neck." She wasn't one of those who criticize, but don't do anything to make a situation better. She went up to Mount Tabor with the army.

If you drive through the broad valley of Jezreel today, you can see at the eastern end of it the rounded hilltop where the troops were to gather. The Hebrew word for *gather* (4:6) implies gathering secretly. But, not surprisingly, the news got to Sisera, captain of the enemy hosts. "Then they told Sisera that Barak the son of Abinoam had gone up to Mount Tabor. And Sisera called together all his chariots, 900 iron chariots, and all the people who were with him, from Harosheth-hagoyim to the River Kishon" (4:12-13).

That's what you call overreaction. Sisera called out his entire military force to stand up to a few weak and pitifully equipped Israelites. But God had promised, "I will draw out to you Sisera . . . I will give him into your hand" (4:7). God wanted the stage set so that all would know the victory was His, not man's.

So the entire force of 900 chariots left the iron foundry town of Harosheth, at the far western end of the valley of Jezreel. Deborah saw the chariots moving out to the Kishon River. We can imagine the terror of Barak, as he measured his military force against that of Sisera. Then Deborah said, " 'Arise! For this is the day in which the Lord has given Sisera into your hands; behold, the Lord has gone out before you.' So Barak went down from Mount Tabor with 10,000 men following him" (4:14).

What made Deborah choose that exact moment? The Israelites were safe from the iron chariots as long as they were gathered on Mount Tabor. How could they dare venture onto the valley floor, where any army with chariots could reign supreme? It was for this that Barak needed Deborah—to tell him God's strategy.

The Kishon River didn't offer much impediment to iron chariots during the late spring and summer months. After the winter and spring rains ended, it could become just a wadi, a dry riverbed, three or four feet deep.

The time might have been late spring, with the Kishon and its tributary streams looking pretty insignificant to Sisera. And maybe Deborah saw some storm clouds forming. Or maybe God spoke to her with a still small voice. We don't know. At any rate, Barak accepted Deborah's challenge and moved. He dared to do what

Israel had never previously risked—come to grips with the dreaded enemy on the plain.

Here we have to turn to Deborah's song of victory to find out what happened:

> Lord, when Thou didst go out from Seir,
> When Thou didst march from the field of Edom,
> The earth quaked, the heavens also dripped,
> Even the clouds dripped water (Jud. 5:4).

The Bible records in various other places that God acted through the thunderstorm, moving in power and splendor to help His people. (See Josh. 10:11; 1 Sam. 7:10; Ps. 18:9-15.)

In 1940 the whole British army was trapped on the mainland of Europe, ready to be wiped out by Hitler's panzer divisions. It seemed they were doomed, and that the war would be over, with Hitler victorious. But England gathered all her little boats, a heavy fog shrouded the channel, and the army was rescued. An armada of private fishing and pleasure boats carried the soldiers across the channel. Without the fog, the army would have been destroyed from the air.

The Battle

In the time of Deborah, God caused a heavy rain, perhaps later in the season than usual, to swell the Kishon. The iron chariots became worse than useless in the flood plain. This kind of situation was repeated when Napoleon defeated the Turkish army at the Battle of Mount Tabor on April 16, 1799.

"And the Lord routed Sisera and all his chariots and all his army, with the edge of the sword before Barak; and Sisera alighted from his chariot and fled away on foot. But Barak pursued the chariots and the army as far as Harosheth-hagoyim, and all the army of Sisera fell by the edge of the sword; not even one was left" (Jud. 4:15-16).

The Kishon became a raging torrent, fed by all its tributary streams. With chariots and horses swamped in the mud, Barak could wipe out Jabin's army with the sword. He pushed them back, back toward the place where the River Kishon narrows and deepens as it flows north of Mount Carmel into the Mediterranean. The surging river swept the bodies away. Deborah's song echoed the wild thrashing of Sisera's horses.

Then the horses' hoofs beat,
From the dashing, the dashing of his valiant steeds (Jud. 5:22).

The general, Sisera, saw the rout and decided to save his own skin. Abandoning his chariot, "Sisera fled away on foot to the tent of Jael the wife of Heber the Kenite, for there was peace between Jabin the king of Hazor and the house of Heber the Kenite. And Jael went out to meet Sisera, and said to him, 'Turn aside, my master, turn aside to me! Do not be afraid.' And he turned aside to her into the tent, and she covered him with a rug" (4:17-18).

Sisera asked for a drink of water, and she gave him milk to drink. In her song, Deborah called it curdled milk which is still commonly consumed in that region as *lebben,* or yogurt.

We don't care to read the next part of the story. Jael flouted the law of hospitality sacred among nomads. For to them, the giving and receiving of hospitality guaranteed protection. Yet Jael deceived and then murdered her guest, the already defeated general.

We are not asked to approve of Jael's actions. The account merely tells what happened—how complete was the defeat of the mighty Canaanites. The point is that Barak, military leader of Israel, couldn't claim much credit for the victory. He even lost the honor of killing the Canaanite general. For this was taken care of by a woman, acting on her own wild impulse. All the details of the victory point to the fact that God's strength is made perfect in weakness. He uses a great variety of instruments, some weak, some mighty, to carry out His designs.

Deborah rejoiced that Sisera was dead. He and his people had harassed the Israelites for 20 years. She thanked Jael for helping to free them.

"So God subdued on that day Jabin the king of Canaan before the sons of Israel. And the hand of the sons of Israel pressed heavier and heavier upon Jabin the king of Canaan, until they had destroyed Jabin the king of Canaan" (4:23-24).

Deborah and Barak didn't quit after the initial victory. They pursued the advantage God had given them, and kept pressing until victory over the Canaanites became complete.

A Thankful Leader

How did Deborah account for her own success? In her song of victory, she praised the Lord for avenging Israel, and the people and the leaders for willingly offering themselves.

Deborah rejoiced that the people who formerly couldn't even draw water without being shot at by arrows now could go to the watering places in peace. There they rejoiced in what God had done (Jud. 5:11).

Deborah showed her sense of leadership of the whole nation as she recalled how the different tribes reacted to the crisis. So many had responded, and their voluntary service had come from their hearts.

A pastor who has built up a church of 3,500 members from nothing says of Deborah, "It's amazing. As a leader she did everything right. She demonstrated her genius for leadership in being able to turn a whole nation around. It's not difficult to get out in front of something already going in the right direction. It's much more difficult to reverse an attitude, especially one of fear and discouragement. First she had to gain the people's confidence. Then, like any great leader, she proposed, then executed, then evaluated the response and results. She let people know where they had succeeded and where they had failed."

Not Everyone Fought

Ephraim and Benjamin had come forward, as had Zebulun and Issachar. But not all had responded. Reuben was one of the two and a half tribes who didn't come all the way into the Promised Land but stayed across the Jordan in fertile Gilead. They didn't show up for the battle. The men of Reuben went through a lot of soul-searching in making up their minds. They held meetings, made speeches, passed great resolutions. But in the end, they stayed home with their flocks. They thought of the lambing, sheep-shearing, sheep market and of all the profit they might expect. After all, they themselves were not in danger. The men of Reuben seemed tied to those sheepfolds with unbreakable bonds.

Dan and Asher had failed too in helping the general cause, choosing to stay at home on the seacoast. The shipping trade looked too lucrative to leave. They were busy loading and unloading trading ships, buying and selling, while Zebulun and Naphtali were risking their lives.

And Meroz, a city located in the middle of the fight—that was the worst of all. Its citizens had stayed behind their walls. The angel of the Lord had a special message for them. "Curse Meroz. . . . Utterly curse its inhabitants; because they did not come to the help of the Lord . . . against the warriors" (5:23).

Deborah left all these thoughts behind to rejoice in God's victory. Those who didn't come forward lost the opportunity of seeing God fight for them. Deborah rejoiced at the change back to normal living for her people. She wondered at the leadership God had given to her. "The peasantry ceased, they ceased in Israel, until I, Deborah, arose, until I arose, a mother in Israel" (5:7).

A Mother in Israel

A mother—what an ideal for leadership! A mother takes upon herself the needs of others. Deborah had a parent heart for every son and daughter of Israel. A mother cherishes every child, strong or weak, gifted or handicapped. A mother seeks only the best for those she loves. She doesn't push herself. She nurtures, encourages, guides, rebukes—as love dictates.

That was Deborah. Few of us are called upon to lead a nation, but we can all seek to develop a mother's heart. We don't need children of our own to do that. Other people's children, young people, adults in their prime, old people, all need mothering. Like Deborah, we can seek to be people who will make others feel stronger just for knowing us.

Some 30 percent of all households in the United States consist of two persons—a husband and wife. This includes childless couples, as well as those whose children are grown. Due to advances in modern medicine, women no longer have to bear six or eight

children to bring two or three to maturity. Also, life expectancy
has greatly lengthened. Today's women can expect to have many
years of good health after their children leave home. What will
they do with those years?

Deborah, a mother in Israel, speaks to all of us. She challenges
us to grow strong in the Lord, then to use our strength to respond
to needs we see all around us. We need many Deborahs, for the
Canaanites are still in the land.

Thus let all Thine enemies perish, O Lord;
But let those who love Him,
Be like the rising of the sun in its might (Jud. 5:31).

The sun rises with steady progress. It proceeds on its appointed
course, whether seen or not seen. It shines on, independent of
circumstances, even when half the world is in darkness.

Deborah comes down to us through history as one who rose like
the sun, inexorably. She illumined a whole nation. She seemingly
came from nowhere, and attained the height of first in the nation,
a mother in Israel. She stood out as counselor, judge, strategist,
inspired leader, and prophetess. Even the setting sun of her career
shines in a halo of selflessness. She directed attention to those who
had helped her, and gave all the glory to God.

"But God has chosen the foolish things of the world to shame
the wise . . . the weak things . . . to shame the things which are
strong, and the base things of the world and the despised . . . the
things that are not . . . that no man should boast before God"
(1 Cor. 1:27-29).

"And the land was undisturbed for 40 years" (Jud. 5:31). That's
what Deborah accomplished for her people—more than a generation of peace.

2
How to Combine
Business with Godliness

Kitty and Carrie, unmarried sisters, worked as businesswomen in Chicago. They also made an impact on several generations of children, including me. As leaders in the Primary Department of our church, they inspired me to memorize many basic Bible verses. Their influence—and those Bible verses—are still with me.

You may have benefited from women like the biblical Lydia. Perhaps you are a Lydia. But who was Lydia? She's mentioned in only three verses of the Bible. But from those verses, and their context, we know that she was a woman of prayer, a businesswoman, a believer, a householder, and a hostess. Historically Lydia stands out as Paul's first convert in Europe. She made her impact as a single woman. Of households in the United States, something like 20 percent are made up of single persons.

Luke, in the Book of Acts, described Lydia as he first met her. He, Silas, and Timothy were with Paul at the time. It was Paul's first Sabbath Day in Europe when he met "a certain woman named Lydia . . . a worshiper of God" (Acts 16:14).

How did these people "happen" to meet? A group of women who believed in God had been getting together for prayer. They met every Sabbath on the banks of the Gangites River outside of Philippi. Lydia, a Gentile, must have been the kind of person who thirsts for God. "As the deer pants for the water brooks, so my soul pants for Thee, O God. My soul thirsts for God, for the living God" (Ps. 42:1-2). Her kind has existed down through the ages—women and men who intuitively turn to the best they know, and pray for more knowledge.

But if those women believed in the God of the Hebrews, why weren't they in a synagogue on the Sabbath Day? Because there was no synagogue in the Roman city of Philippi. No synagogue meant there were not even 10 Jewish men in the whole city, for to organize a synagogue required 10 men.

Where, then, did Lydia get her faith? Maybe she brought it from Thyatira, her home city. At any rate, she had espoused the Hebrew faith with its high moral standards, its lofty conception of a God of holiness and love.

Today you can look over the ruins of Philippi. You can also go a short way into the countryside and stand beside a beautiful little river, banked by trees and low hills. There you can imagine those women thirsting for God as they read from the Old Testament, as they prayed for God to reveal Himself more fully to them.

During the weeks or months the women met and prayed, a man named Paul was traveling in Asia Minor. It was his second missionary journey, and he was encountering one difficulty after another. First he split up with his old friend and supporter Barnabas, in a disagreement about Barnabas' nephew, John Mark. John Mark had turned back on the first missionary trip, and Paul was sick of him, and didn't want him along again. So Barnabas took Mark, and Paul started off with Silas.

Things went all right for a while. Paul and Silas revisited the churches Paul had already started. They had a happy find at Lystra—young Timothy had developed well as a believer. Paul invited Timothy to join him and Silas. It was a good choice, for Timothy continued with Paul for practically the rest of Paul's life.

But then things started going badly. As the party of three tried to enter new regions to start churches, one thing after another blocked them. When they tried to go west, they were "forbidden by the Holy Spirit to speak the Word in Asia" (Acts 16:6). When they tried to go north, "the Spirit of Jesus did not permit them" (Acts 16:7). Paul must have felt stymied. He probably thought that he of all people should know the leading of the Holy Spirit. They were stopped from going anywhere except down to the shore to Troas. From there he could look across the Hellespont and see outlines of the shore of Europe.

Maybe Paul was sick, and thereby prevented from going to the other places. We don't know. At any rate, Luke, a doctor, joined the group in Troas. Perhaps it was Luke, a Greek, who told Paul about opportunities for the Gospel in Greece. For "a vision appeared to Paul in the night: a certain man of Macedonia . . . appealing to him, and saying, 'Come over into Macedonia, and help us' " (Acts 16:9).

During all this time, Lydia and her friends had kept on gathering by the riverbank, their place of prayer (Acts 16:13). They didn't know anything about Paul, but they certainly wanted fuller light.

After Paul's vision, the group decided to go into Macedonia, believing that God had called them to preach the Gospel there (Acts 16:10).

For a few days things went well for Paul and his party. They found a sailing vessel which was going across, and made the trip in only two days. The wind was at their backs. Later on, the same trip would take five days. So this time they must have concluded they had found God's will at last. He was making things easy for them.

We're all too inclined to equate God's will with seeing everything go well. But Jesus did God's will, and things certainly didn't go well all the time for Him. Neither did they for Paul. Paul considered suffering, hardship, and inconvenience as part of his mission.

Paul in Philippi

The ship landed at Neapolis, the port of Philippi. Neapolis is now called Kavalla. They traveled, probably on foot, along the Egnation Way the eight miles to Philippi. That great Roman road crossed Macedonia, the northern part of Greece, connecting East with West, the Aegean Sea with the Adriatic. The Egnation Way, like other Roman roads, knew the tramp of infantry legions, as well as the pounding of hooves of cavalry divisions. It carried the burdens of commerce, as well as travelers like Paul and his companions. The Romans constructed the Egnation Way so solidly, of great blocks of stone, that parts of it still exist. In some places you can walk on it and see the ruts worn in the stone by carts and carriages of Roman times.

Always a strategist, Paul saw Philippi as the place to start. Luke explained why. It was "a leading city of the district of Macedonia, a Roman colony" (Acts 16:12).

Philippi's location on the Egnation Way meant the Gospel could be carried to many places. Philip of Macedon had founded Philippi four centuries earlier as a fortified city. The great battle in 42 B.C. that ended the Roman Republic and inaugurated the Empire was fought on the plains near Philippi. After the battle, Antony and Octavian settled their veterans there and made Philippi a Roman colony. That meant its citizens enjoyed all the rights and privileges of Rome itself.

So the Philippians clung jealously to their Roman traditions and resented any encroachments from outsiders. They accused Paul and Silas: "These men are throwing our city into confusion, being Jews, and are proclaiming customs which it is not lawful for us to accept or to observe, being Romans" (Acts 16:20-21).

No wonder so few Jews lived there. Paul must have felt discouraged. He always started his work in a synagogue, where he could expect to find people who believed in God, who knew the Old Testament.

But Paul was willing to be led by the Holy Spirit in new ways. Even though he had found one method that worked, he wasn't averse to learning others. Sometimes we're all too ready to say, "But we've always done it this way."

Paul and his party spent some time learning the city and getting adjusted. On our first visit to Europe, Bart and I traveled, as Paul did, on faith, courage, wits, and very little money. When we arrived in a new city, after finding the cheapest place to stay, we'd spend the first day getting our bearings. That meant finding maps and travel folders, bus and subway schedules. We couldn't afford expensive tours, but the folders told us what the tour groups saw. Then we got around by bus, subway, and on foot to see the sights. We met a lot of interesting people and had many adventures. I've always understood just why Paul spent some days getting his bearings. A new city can feel overwhelming. Paul on first arrival met with complete indifference to him and his dreams.

In many strange places on our travels, Bart and I have hunted up a church—or the nearest thing to what we thought of as a church. When Sunday comes, we always want to worship with God's people.

Likewise, Luke wrote, "On the Sabbath Day we went outside the gate to a riverside, where we were supposing that there would be a place of prayer" (Acts 16:13).

How did they know to go to the river? During the years of captivity in Babylon, Jews established the custom of meeting by rivers. "By the rivers of Babylon, there we sat down and wept, when we remembered Zion" (Ps. 137:1). In their dispersion throughout the ancient world, Jews learned to find each other at a river, if there was no synagogue.

At the riverside outside Philippi, Paul probably expected to find at least a few men. In his vision, a man beckoned him over to Macedonia.

But here among the trees, by the bubbling stream, he found only women. That's all God was offering him as a base for all of Europe. Should he turn around and go back? Should he figure he had misread God's leading? I've always liked Paul for sitting right down with those women and proceeding as if they were a whole synagogue.

How many churches have been built on the prayers of only a few people? We spent 13 wonderful years at a church that previously had had practically no Gospel ministry. One woman in the congregation had prayed—diligently—for a spiritual ministry. The Spirit "constrained" us to go there.

"And a certain woman named Lydia, from the city of Thyatira, a seller of purple fabrics, a worshiper of God, was listening" (Acts 16:14).

Besides being a worshiper of God, this Lydia was a business-woman. She came from a city in western Asia Minor, in the Roman province of Asia. Thyatira, like Philippi, was an important point on the Roman road system. It was a manufacturing center, famous for its dyeing industry. A large town, Akhisar, still stands on the same site.

Lydia was probably the overseas agent of a Thyatiran manufacturer. *Purple* could refer to the dye itself, or more likely to woolen or linen goods dyed a rich hue. The dye was a secretion of a shellfish, which when crushed yielded the rich color. That color could vary all the way from blue-purple to scarlet. Sometimes threads were dyed, then woven into varicolored fabrics. Other times the cloth itself was dyed. It might be immersed several times to make the color deeper.

Of course it took a great many shellfish to dye a piece of cloth. The whole process was so costly that scarlet or purple could be worn only by kings or wealthy people. The color spoke of rank and nobility. Lydia was probably one of the most successful and influential women in Philippi.

And God had prepared her heart for Paul. "The Lord opened her heart to respond to the things spoken by Paul. And when she and her household had been baptized . . ." (Acts 16:14-15). That one heart was enough.

Dorothy

Dorothy, a modern Lydia, heard her pastor in Denver say that only one out of eight people in Denver went to church. She knew no one on her block attended church. Her pastor said that he sometimes went up to a mountain overlooking Denver and prayed for the whole city.

Said Dorothy, "I thought that if one person on each block were praying for each person on her block, the whole city would be prayed for, person by person. I didn't know everyone on my block. But I started praying for the people in the house with the red door, those with the special shrubbery. Soon I decided I needed to meet them. To do so, I would accept when someone called to ask me to collect for a good cause. Or I'd simply introduce myself. Or I'd take some baked goods over to a new neighbor. Or I'd have a coffee and invite some in to meet a new neighbor.

"Soon seven of us—five Christians and two others—decided to

start a Bible study group. When it grew to 15 or 20, we split into two groups. When I moved three years later, 80 percent of the people on our block had been born again. The one little prayer and Bible study group had grown and split until about 200 people were involved.

"I resolved that wherever I moved I would do the same thing—pray for all the people on my block."

I learned about Dorothy's prayers when I met someone who had just joined our church. The new member said, "There are so many people on our block coming to this church, I can't understand it."

I traced the mystery down, found Dorothy at the bottom of it. She walks up and down the block praying for the people in each house.

Lydia

That was Lydia. She prayed; then when she heard the Gospel, she believed. When she believed, she acted. Lydia was baptized. Baptism in that day meant stepping out. Today being baptized is the respectable thing to do. We have to think of additional ways to make ourselves known as Christians.

But to Lydia baptism meant proclaiming to the world that she espoused this new teaching. Lydia didn't wait to see what effect her new faith might have on her business. She didn't evaluate if her fashionable clients would think more or less of her if she proclaimed her faith in Christ. Though a successful business-woman, she hadn't sold her soul to business. Her relationship to God came first.

The first thing Lydia did was witness to her household. What did the household consist of? We don't know. Lydia could have been a single woman, with a household of servants and retainers to assist in running her business. She could have been a widow. We read nothing of any husband or children.

Women seem to have had somewhat more freedom in that locality than in other parts of the world. Luke spoke of "the prominent women" of Thessalonica and of Berea, both in eastern Macedonia. More than a few of these, said Luke, accepted the Gospel (Acts 17:4, 12).

We learn something about Lydia through seeing her whole household accept baptism so readily. They must have loved and respected her, and been used to looking to her for wise decisions.

After the members of her household were baptized as believers, Lydia invited the four evangelists to stay with her. Now you may think it takes some doing to entertain one evangelist, much less four! But Lydia wanted to drink in more of what she had heard. She wanted to grow in her faith. One way to grow is to be around people who are farther ahead in the Christian life.

To hear and accept the Gospel is like being born—the vitally important first step for life. But life won't last long if a baby doesn't find food right away. Lydia was hungry and she saw to it that she had some spiritual food close at hand. She was ready to turn her living arrangements upside down to get started in this new life.

To begin living the new kind of life that goes with being born again requires change. We have to be ready to rearrange our schedules, give up our convenience, turn our lives inside out.

In inviting those missionaries to stay in her home, Lydia not only provided for her own spiritual needs. She also launched the church in Europe. We can picture Paul and the others meeting and talking with new believers in Lydia's comfortable home. The church probably continued to meet in Lydia's house after Paul, Silas, and Timothy left Philippi.

As long as Paul remained in Philippi, Luke traveled with him. But Luke seems to have stayed behind when Paul left. Philippi was quite a medical center. Maybe Luke worked there as a doctor. Maybe he stayed to help the infant church. Another "we" section in Acts occurs when Paul returned to Philippi, indicating that Luke rejoined him there.

Notice the warmth of Lydia's hospitality. She not only invited Paul and his co-workers to stay in her house. She constrained them, prevailed upon them, persuaded them. It's one thing to say, "Stop in and see me sometime," and something else to say, "Come right now, today," or to set a certain date. It's one thing to say to a sick person, "Let me know if you need anything," and something else to say, "I'm bringing in a hot meal tonight." It's one thing to say to your pastor, "Let me know if I can help," and another to say, "I will entertain the next missionaries who come." Or, "I will come to the church tomorrow to help get the church records straightened out." Or, "I will teach that Sunday School class that is without a teacher."

Lydia urged and insisted. Paul apparently held back. Maybe he felt embarrassed about accepting hospitality so quickly. There were all too many religious people in those days going around getting well paid for quackery. Paul refused to accept any material help at all from the Corinthians, for fear his motives would be suspect. But the Philippians always seemed to have a special relationship with him.

Perhaps Lydia set the tone of that relationship. Later, while Paul was working in Corinth and was in need, the Philippians sent him financial assistance (2 Cor. 8:1-4). He couldn't always earn enough from his tentmaking.

And when Paul was in prison in Rome, 10 years later, Pastor Epaphroditus nearly died making the journey to Rome with money from the Philippian church. Paul wrote his letter to the Philippians as a thank-you note for that. He admitted he really needed the money. So they were like family to him, able to help without embarrassing him. In the Philippian letter he thanked God for their "participation in the Gospel from the first day until now" (Phil. 1:5). Paul never forgot the warm hospitality that Lydia offered him at the very start.

Sally, a present-day believer, feels that hospitality is part of her ministry for Christ. She entertains missionaries, and large and small groups from the church. She kept a new minister and his wife and two children for four weeks while they waited to move into their own home. Says Sally, "Keep them coming. I love people so much, I consider it a privilege to entertain for Christ. Doing so enlarges my own family, my circle of friends, my world. I learn so much from these people. When they stay overnight, I really get to know them; I've lived with them. I feel the key to successful entertaining is flexibility, being willing to give up control of my kitchen and let people help and feel at home. I have to fit into other lifestyles. We want to share what God has given to us. We're really just taking care of it for Him."

But that's not all about Lydia. Paul and his friends, quietly going through the city on their way to prayer, got involved in difficulties. "As we were going to the place of prayer, a certain slave-girl having a spirit of divination met us, who was bringing her masters much profit by fortune-telling. Following after Paul and us, she kept crying out, saying, 'These men are bond-servants of the Most High God, who are proclaiming to you the way of salvation'" (Acts 16:16-17).

Paul found it distressing to have such a person speaking out for him, and in such an inappropriate way. So he commanded the spirit of divination to come out of the girl. It did, but that meant her owners had lost their means of income. So they stirred up trouble until Paul and Silas—the two Jews of the foursome—were thrown into prison.

There the Roman jailer and his family were converted, and Paul was released. But he certainly wasn't a popular figure in Philippi. He had interfered with somebody's livelihood. Lydia could easily have wanted to pretend she didn't know him. The whole ruckus definitely wouldn't help her business.

But Lydia was no doubt praying for the two in prison. For when they were freed, they "entered into the house of Lydia, and when they saw the brethren, they encouraged them and departed" (Acts 16:40).

Christ came first with Lydia. She turned over to Him everything she had—her house, her business, her privacy. Paul launched the whole missionary enterprise for Europe through one prepared heart—Lydia's.

Are you a Lydia?

3
How to
Gain Your Rights

A father of seven sons was commiserating with one who had just
acquired his third child—a third son. The young father and his wife
had hoped for a girl. "I can give you the formula for getting a
daughter. Just keep on going," said the father of seven sons. His
eighth child is a girl.

It wasn't always like this—fathers genuinely wanting daughters.
Ancient Israel was a strongly patriarchal society where men held
the power. The birth of a son meant someone to carry on the
family name and identity. It meant someone to inherit the family
property. A daughter was valued only for the work she could
contribute. Her husband would pay her parents a sum of money in
order to marry her, because she was a working asset. But in the
end, she'd be absorbed into her husband's family, lost to her own.

"Now Zelophehad the son of Hepher had no sons, but only
daughters" (Num. 26:33). A real tragedy for Zelophehad. Five
times he hoped for a male heir and five times he was disappointed.
Yet he apparently loved those daughters, and planted in them a
love and appreciation for him, and for their family tradition. They
wanted to carry it on.

"And the names of the daughters of Zelophehad were Mahlah,
Noah, Hoglah, Milcah, and Tirzah" (Num. 26:33). Each is named
in Scripture. In God's sight, each was important.

God knows each one of us by name. Every one of us, however unimportant in the world's eyes, can make an impact for God. These girls demonstrated the power of simply asking for a just right. You and I should not fail to ask for something God in His justice would want us to have.

The Israelites had spent 40 years wandering about the wilderness. Marking out the campground, unpacking, and setting up tents meant work for everyone. The women must have kept busy gathering sticks, building fires, gathering the manna and cooking it in different ways to give some variety to the diet. Clothing had to be cared for, tents cleaned, waste disposed of, the grounds kept clean. Children had to be bathed and fed, borne and buried.

Then when the signal came, women had to take down the tents, pack up all those household goods and move on.

A modern woman finds it a burden to move back and forth from a city to a country home every week or two. Says Doris, "My husband is under such pressure as head of his company that he just has to get away. He's a different person as soon as he leaves the city. But I feel as though I can never settle down and complete anything; I'm always tired out from being constantly on the run. I just never feel I can undertake much that I want to do because I'm always arranging for the next move."

Other women feel in a constant state of upheaval because of their husbands' frequent transfers from one city to another. Buying a new house, selling the old one, refurnishing, settling in, and getting adjusted in new surroundings uses up all their creative energy.

Those women in the wilderness must have found life endlessly tiring, as women with small children find life exhausting today—even with comforts and conveniences. Certainly women's attention then was glued to the routines of life. Not many thought about their rights, for men had all the rights.

The whole nation, in its ponderous moving from place to place, at last arrived in view of the Promised Land. Excitement about the inheritance each would receive crackled through the camp. Male representatives of all the families were jockeying for position, for each wanted to claim his just share.

A Household of Women

One family of five orphaned daughters had no male to make claim for them (Num. 27:1). They were descendants of the mighty Joseph who ruled Egypt, members of the second largest tribe, Manasseh, which was named after one of Joseph's two sons. But their father had died in the wilderness. So these daughters banded together for courage to make their claim. Undoubtedly, they found in each other companionship and mutual support.

Today, approximately four percent of American households consist of relatives other than spouses living together. These, like the daughters of Zelophehad, find themselves held together by a common background. Companionship, pooled resources, and mutual strengthening constitute reason enough to stay together.

When Dorothy was 15, her mother died. A year later her father moved the four children to another city where he was working. When the father's work took him to still another city, the young people stayed. They were on their own, lonely strangers in that city.

"We got along fine," says Dorothy. "My mother had taught us to love each other and we really depended on each other. We had always gone to church back East, but here we went to one church and no one spoke to us. My sister, Gertrude, who was always the leader, said, 'Why don't we try that little church across the street?'

"When the people in that church saw four young people come in, they could hardly wait till the service was over to surround us. From that moment on, we were part of the church. We went to all the young people's activities and met young people whom we dated.

"Another thing that helped us get along together—we were all trained to work. My sister and I worked full-time; the two boys worked part-time, while both still in school. We all helped with the housework.

"My father was going to pay the rent, but after he married again, that ended. We had to pay the rent ourselves, had to help each other. When I had a sudden appendectomy, and couldn't pay for it, my sister did. When my brother bought a car, then lost his job, I continued the payments on his car. That first spring when we thought my father was going to pay the rent, I had saved up enough money to buy a new spring outfit. I used it to pay rent—and was glad I had the money. The amount was just enough. My brothers did all they could, but we had to help them through school. When my sister lost her money in a bank failure, we all helped her.

"We grew very close as we helped each other through a difficult time. Eventually, we all married Christians whom we met in our church."

The male cousins of those daughters of Zelophehad weren't interested in their cause. The daughters were on their own. Perhaps the cousins feared it would cut into their own portions of land for the women to get a share. And five women didn't need to be feared. They were only women, utterly without power.

But those women possessed decisiveness and courage. They wanted to break away from the conventional notion that they should tamely submit to injustice.

Ask to Receive

The industrial and medical revolutions made increased freedom for women a possibility. But women's rights movements have made that freedom a reality. For women had to ask.

Women didn't have the vote till they asked for it. They were not admitted to colleges and universities till someone asked. They weren't admitted to law or medical school till some woman applied. They didn't get into management positions till some had courage enough to appeal for fair opportunities.

"And they stood before Moses and before Eleazar the priest and before the leaders and all the congregation, at the doorway of the tent of meeting" (Num. 27:2).

The place of women in a society is determined by many factors, such as custom, religion, politics, and economics. In that social situation, how did those girls ever get up the courage to ask for something women had never laid claim to before? Didn't they worry about how they would be received before the tribal leaders, before the congregation? How would they ever get husbands, if they pushed themselves forward? If they appeared to break out of the accepted pattern for women?

A young woman completing her master's degree was trying to decide between accepting a teaching job, or continuing at the University of Chicago to earn her doctor's degree. Her father wanted his daughter's happiness, so he asked her, "Do you want a husband, or do you want a Ph.D. degree?"

"I want a husband," she answered, in a little-girl voice.

"If that's the case," said her father, "then I would advise you to take the teaching position. That particular one offers a good opportunity for meeting a husband. If you get your Ph.D. degree first, you may never find a husband." She found the husband; then both of them got Ph.D. degrees.

Many a woman in today's world has curbed her ambition, given up getting an advanced degree, limited her success in business—to get a husband. Women fear that personal aggressiveness or success may prove too threatening to a man. But after such a woman marries, the sense of unrealized potential may generate serious conflict.

Those daughters of Zelophehad ignored any fears they had. They discussed their needs and took thought of the nature of God. Then they gathered up their courage, and appeared in the open space before the tabernacle in the center of the camp.

God encourages us to ask in order to receive. Those women who had no natural protector openly brought their cause before Moses, and so before God. "In whom we have boldness and confident access through faith in Him" (Eph. 3:12). Approaching God means knowing that no one is unimportant in His sight. It also means being willing to take no for an answer as well as yes.

Wait to Receive

Many women have eventually gained a much-wanted freedom by being willing to wait for it. Sometimes a wife wants to go back to school, get a job, undertake volunteer work—do something on her own. She discovers her husband's poor faltering ego can't take it. He married her with a need to feel superior to her.

But she need not give up. As he matures, and she builds up his self-image and self-confidence, the time may come when he can feel really happy about her development. He may discover he really wants the companionship of an equal. However, if she pushes or demands, she may destroy him, or their marriage.

Cynthia, a high school graduate, helped her husband through college, medical school, and specialization. He clearly regarded her as an inferior, and she chafed under his attitude, feeling restless and occasionally resentful. He regarded her position as the proper one for a Christian wife. One day in church he heard a discussion about women in the Bible who had, under God, developed and used their gifts. His viewpoint changed. His wife embarked on a course at a local college and in four years graduated magna cum laude. Her achievement changed their relationship for the better as he developed a new respect for her.

Those daughters of Zelophehad simply asked. Quietly, they stated their case. Their father had passed away in the wilderness, as part of the generation that had to die before Israel could enter the Promised Land. His generation was too lacking in courage to claim the Land. Only a generation reared in desert conditions could leave the slave mentality of Egypt behind.

The daughters of Zelophehad certainly showed themselves free of any slave mentality. They had thought out their case, they had an argument. "Our father . . . was not among the company of those who gathered themselves together against the Lord in the company of Korah" (Num. 27:3). He wasn't part of Korah's rebellion. All those rebels were condemned to die specifically for their sin of refusing the authority of Moses. So the five daughters justly had rights, they felt, along with the male heirs of their father's brothers.

"Why should the name of our father be withdrawn from among his family because he had no son? Give us a possession among our father's brothers" (Num. 27:4).

Their request was out in the open. Would the heavens fall? The tabernacle collapse? The Holy Place burst into flame and devour them? The males standing about mob or stone them?

Moses was a patient man. He'd listened to all kinds of complaints, murmurings, injustices, suggestions. In this case too he listened and then brought their cause before God.

An astonishing answer came. The whole law changed because five orphaned daughters had the courage to ask. "Then the Lord spoke to Moses, saying, 'The daughters of Zelophehad are right in their statements. You shall surely give them a hereditary possession among their father's brothers . . . you shall speak to the sons of Israel, saying, "If a man dies and has no son, then you shall transfer his inheritance to his daughter"'" (Num. 27:6-8).

Women couldn't inherit in other Near Eastern countries. Now they could in Israel. A God of equity showed His disregard for mere legal rights. Henceforward we see this new law in operation in the Old Testament, in the Book of Ruth and in the prophets. Women could hold title to property.

Give Preference

It has taken women a long time to recapture some of the rights they exercised in ancient Israel. Time and time again in Israel's history, God made exceptions to the general social pattern in favor of individual women.

Later, the chief fathers of the tribe to which the daughters of Zelophehad belonged saw a problem. They feared that the law that daughters could inherit in the absence of male heirs would mix up the tribal allotments (Num. 36:1-13). Distribution of land for the whole nation was based on tribal allotments. If daughters married into other tribes, bits of land would go with them, and tribal boundaries would become confused.

So a limitation was added to the law for the general good. Daughters who inherited land were to marry men of their own tribe. Then the land would stay in that tribe.

Many a modern child of God has claimed her own rights, yet in love has put a limitation upon herself. A woman who puts God first won't want to ignore the rights of other women, of men, of children, or even of unborn children. She doesn't hate men, nor does she want to infringe upon their freedom or rights—or even on their self-confidence. She lovingly follows the principle to "give preference to one another in honor" (Rom. 12:10).

But a woman has a right to expect the same consideration from a man—father, brother, husband, or even employer. A man who follows Christ should want to see any one of God's creatures realize his or her highest potential.

If God hadn't wanted women to learn calculus, show skill in surgery, lead a nation, run a business, write a poem, or teach a class, He wouldn't have given them such abilities. Not all men can do those things. Neither can all women. But the individuals who can shouldn't be deprived of the opportunity.

Today women feel free to go to college; they apply for jobs that men have usually filled; they submit their efforts in the artistic world. God sees every one of us in terms of potential. He puts no limitation upon us except the limitation of love—whatever truly serves others. At the same time, God's respect for us doesn't depend upon brilliant achievement. It depends upon trusting and following Him. We all need to learn to look at people through God's eyes.

We can thank God for men secure enough to encourage women to their highest development. And for women unselfish enough to encourage men to their highest potential. There is certainly not so much talent abroad in the world that we can afford to see any of it go to waste.

There's no harm in asking. It's a basic principle that works in small matters as well as large. I've discovered it works in small matters of travel. As you go about the world, you get all kinds of astonishing concessions just by a polite inquiry. You want a substitution on the menu, a room with a better view, a side trip on a sight-seeing tour, or a certain guide. I make up my mind ahead of time that I'm not going to fight about whatever is bothering me. I'm not going to demand, or be unpleasant. Somehow life seems too short, the journey too soon over for that. But there's no harm in asking. Sometimes the answer is, "No, we can't do it." But other times the answer is yes.

The principle works in women's rights. We aren't interested

in tearing up society, churning up the church, ripping our families apart, or even unnerving our husbands. But there's no harm in asking.

As we make the men around us feel more secure, they can grant us privileges that won't interfere a particle with their fullest freedom and development.

The daughters of Zelophehad demonstrated the value of gathering up their courage and asking.

4
How to Manage Everything Well

Women work for many different reasons.

"My wife is much happier when she's working at her profession—and I like her to be happy," said a husband with a glow of pride. "So she works part time as a nurse—that keeps her in touch."

"I feel that my wife has brilliant talents. It would be a crime to keep her from using them," said the husband of a woman who teaches in a university.

"I wish I didn't have to work. I'd like to stay home," said a woman who works as a supermarket cashier. "But we just can't make ends meet without my paycheck as well as my husband's."

"I liked the freedom of not having to work," said a wife who works in a real estate office. "But it makes my husband very nervous to feel he's carrying the whole financial load, so I have to work."

About 20 percent of American households consist of families with children at home, with both parents working. More than half of all married women now work. Is that out of line with what the Bible says a home should be?

Not at all. The description of the ideal woman, in Proverbs 31:10-31, shows a wife and mother who can do everything. She supervises all household responsibilities, cares for her children, keeps her husband happy. She helps him get ahead in the world. In addition, she deals successfully in real estate, and runs her own manufacturing business. As if that weren't enough, she also makes her own clothes, always speaks wisely and kindly, and never fails to trust the Lord.

Lest you fold up completely in total discouragement, remember she's an ideal woman—not a flesh-and-blood historical person. She represents all the things that the Hebrews admired in a woman. We can all measure ourselves against her, and try to improve. She challenges us to learn to do a lot of different things, to balance a number of activities at the same time.

A Good Wife

"An excellent wife, who can find? For her worth is far above jewels" (Prov. 31:10). That first phrase is variously translated: "A wife of noble character who can find?" (NIV) "A good wife who can find?" (RSV)

The whole Book of Proverbs is given as advice to a son about how to get along well in this world. It describes various types of women: the loose woman, the adventuress, the harlot; wisdom personified as a woman; the nag, the scold, the quarrelsome wife, the contentious and fretful woman; the foolish and noisy woman, the beautiful woman without discretion. The Book of Proverbs climaxes with this detailed description of what the son is to look for in a wife.

Every young person has a picture in his mind of what he wants in a life partner. A girl wants a Prince Charming who is tall, dark, and handsome. A boy dreams of a girl with golden curls, or of a ravishing redhead. As he gets closer to marriage, he comes to terms with what is available. Some superficial qualities are gladly sacrificed for more essential traits.

This woman in Proverbs 31:10-31 represents a composite of the many good traits a wife might possess. No woman possesses them all. Yet the son is urged to look for as many as possible in choosing his wife. The poem is in the form of an acrostic—22 verses, one for each letter of the Hebrew alphabet, aleph, beth, gimel, daleth, and so on. It could be called the ABC of the perfect wife. In this form, the young man could memorize it and keep in mind all he was to look for.

In choosing a partner from fallible human beings, we look for strengths where we're weak, and don't mind weaknesses where we're strong. Husbands and wives commonly complement each other to achieve well-rounded couple strength.

Certainly the composite picture in Proverbs 31 forms a good directive for bringing up a daughter. Every girl wants to be wanted. How can parents help her become the worthy choice of a good man? How can parents help her to cope with life after she does get married? By training her with this picture from Proverbs in mind. She'll find her own happiness through learning to handle household tasks easily, earn her own living, meet other people's needs, and let God shape her life.

Fear the Lord

"Charm is deceitful, and beauty is vain, but a woman who fears the Lord, she shall be praised" (Prov. 31:30). An article in a woman's magazine described what happened to seven beauties some 20 years after they had been feted. In most cases their lives had gone downhill. The point of the article: don't grieve if you're not an outstanding beauty. Be thankful if you have to learn when young how to build your self-esteem on a more enduring base.

The Bible gives the true base: "The fear of the Lord is the beginning of knowledge" (Prov. 1:7). This remarkable woman of Proverbs possessed an inner strength, and a strong sense of priorities. She shaped her life around her relationship with God.

Smile at the Future

"Strength and dignity are her clothing, and she smiles at the future" (Prov. 31:25). Different periods of history and different social settings have produced different ideals of womanhood: the baby doll, the beauty, the fainting lady, the servant, the chattel, the drudge. But the biblical ideal is a woman of strength who possesses and develops many abilities. "Whatever your hand finds to do, verily, do it with all your might" (Ecc. 9:10).

This woman laughs at the future for two reasons. First, she puts her trust in God. Second, she exercises all the abilities and strengths God has given her to take care of her family's needs.

Teach with Kindness

"She opens her mouth in wisdom, and the teaching of kindness is on her tongue" (Prov. 31:26). The virtuous woman speaks with wisdom. This means she has taken time to think, to learn, to grow.

I've discovered that if I don't take time to put something into my mind, nothing very worthwhile comes out. No matter how busy I am, I must find time for my own soul's growth. At one time, I hired a baby-sitter for a couple of hours a day so I would have time to study. The baby-sitter expressed surprise. She'd never heard of anybody who paid money so she could sit down in her own living room.

If you don't take what seems like time for yourself, you'll get so empty and drained you'll feel like a dry husk. And a dry husk isn't much satisfaction to anyone.

So a woman who wants to keep a busy life in balance starts with her own inner strength. It takes time to keep alive a relationship with God. "By wisdom a house is built. And by understanding it is established; and by knowledge the rooms are filled with all precious and pleasant riches" (Prov. 24:3-4).

Any real estate salesman would rather sell a furnished than an unfurnished house. The rooms look smaller in an empty house, and every flaw shows. A woman needs a well-furnished mind. The Bible offers all good things to fill the chambers of the mind.

Time for yourself, whatever you need for your own soul's growth, is not selfish. For your family's sake, see to your own development.

Do Good

"The heart of her husband trusts in her, and he will have no lack of gain. She does him good and not evil all the days of her life" (Prov. 31:11-12). In building her house, this ideal wife first of all establishes a relationship of trust with her husband. He knows he can trust her word. He can trust her with his checkbook and charge cards. She won't run up bills that he can never pay.

She meets his needs on a deep level of psychological security. He can safely confide in her his disappointments, his hurts, his insecurities. He knows she won't use these things against him to destroy him. She keeps his confidences confidential. She's very tender of his ego, and does all she can to build up his self-image. She shows her belief in him no matter what.

He also knows he can trust her to carry her end of the load so that he can carry his. And she'll do all this throughout her life—not just at the beginning of their marriage.

An ideal wife is ideal for her own husband, not necessarily for another man. Each man is different, with individual needs. The ideal wife won't insist on doing for her husband what he doesn't want done. She's flexible. She won't persist in a certain pattern because that's what she was taught, or that's what her father wanted, or that's what some article or book said was the way to please a husband. She'll study her own man as a person and talk things over with him.

. One woman had been married 12 years when she learned her husband had gotten a young girl pregnant. "I worked so hard at being a wife. I scrubbed and cleaned, I baked, even made my own bread, besides helping in our printing business, really running it. I thought all that was what was important in a wife—it's what I had been taught. After the divorce I realized I just hadn't met his psychological or physical needs."

A good wife first of all meets the deep heart needs of her husband.

Help Your Husband

"Her husband is known in the gates, when he sits among the elders of the land" (Prov. 31:23). The ideal wife also manages to find time to help her husband get ahead. Likewise, he should help her find fulfillment. Other parts of the Bible make it clear he's to put her needs before his own. (See Eph. 5:25 ff.) The Scriptures make clear that both husband and wife are to build each other up, never tear each other down. Couples working as a team can accomplish amazing things, individually and together, for God and family. Each multiplies the other's effectiveness.

Wives help their husbands get ahead in many different ways. One husband needs a wife to serve as a wailing wall. He needs to get all his problems "ventilated," as the psychologists say. He can see solutions better after he's talked his problems out, and has listened to his wife's viewpoint. Sometimes it's an advantage for her not to be too closely involved in his affairs. Then she can see his problems with some objectivity.

Another husband brings none of his problems home. He prefers to forget the office or shop, and wants a wife who makes life fun and relaxing at home.

Another wants a wife to take him into a wider world culturally or spiritually than he has time or strength to pursue on his own.

One husband wants actual help with his business, perhaps in bookkeeping, answering the telephone, driving a tractor, or taking care of customers at certain hours. Another wants a wife to help him by staying out of his business. She must let him run it his own way, not her way.

It's all part of studying your own husband, figuring out his individual needs, and meeting them.

Work with Your Hands

"She looks for wool and flax, and works with her hands in delight" (Prov. 31:13). The next area of this illustrious wife's perfect functioning: caring for her household. A good wife doesn't dodge working with her hands. She doesn't let dishes pile up in the sink, nor dust gather behind the furniture. No one has to urge her to work. She goes in search of it. In those days wool and flax were spun and woven in the home. She didn't seek to escape work by refusing to bring unspun wool and flax into the house. I suppose the modern equivalent is a woman's willingness to prepare food from basic ingredients. My husband will not eat TV dinners, but is quite content with anything I have prepared and put into the freezer. So I keep homemade chili, soups, various things in the freezer for the days when I can't face cooking a meal, or get home late, or have to be away.

"She is like merchant ships; she brings her food from afar" (Prov. 31:14). The ideal wife shops wisely. She makes weekly or twice-weekly trips to the supermarket, and plans her meals around whatever is a good buy. She doesn't run out to the local delicatessen for expensive tidbits or prepared foods a half hour before mealtime.

"She rises also while it is still night, and gives food to her household, and portions to her maidens" (Prov. 31:15). Now I personally am not fond of rising while it is yet night. I would just as soon excise that verse from the passage. But I do know wives who rise up early. One said, "I get up every morning with my husband at five o'clock to see him off to work, and I stay up. I think it's important that I be tired at night when he wants to go to bed."

Another wife works in public relations for a car company. She leaves her toddler at nursery school each morning before she drives 45 minutes to arrive at work at eight o'clock. That means arising while it is yet night.

But my pastor husband, like real estate or insurance salesmen, pharmacists, or factory workers on the late shift, is out every evening in his work. So I simply turn the day around. I get a head start on the day's work the night before, and have a little more relaxed beginning in the morning.

We all know it takes planning to provide food for a household, sometimes some advance preparation. Just once I visited in a home where mealtime came and went, and nothing happened. A home without food is an unappealing place. We all like to see food appear at regular intervals. A well-stocked larder can help to keep children as well as husbands at home.

As to providing tasks for our maidens, most of us are not burdened with servants standing around. Translated into modern terms, we see this ideal woman as a good manager. She gets the clothes into and out of the automatic washer and dryer at the proper time, not after her husband and children reach a state of frenzy with no clean clothes to wear. She also gets dishes into and out of the dishwasher at the proper time, not after the family runs out of dishes. She allocates tasks to her children and to her husband as the balance of burdens requires. But she takes the ultimate responsibility for running the household.

Spend Wisely

"She considers a field and buys it; from her earnings she plants a vineyard" (Prov. 31:16). Having mastered all household functions, this woman moves into the area of investment in real estate. She's smart. She's able to figure out a good buy. And she's made some money so that she can develop a vineyard. This wife seems to move gradually from the home to the outside world in her business activities.

Today's working wife more often starts with the job which she holds before marriage. She must take on responsibility for a home after she gets married.

Between 1950 and 1975 the number of employed married women, living with their husbands and with children under 18 at home, increased by 217 percent.

Parents can help their daughters to carry this dual role by teaching them housework as children. In today's world, management of the machinery of life should be taught to both boys and girls until it becomes second nature. When men and women divide the responsibility of earning a living, marriage goes more smoothly if they also divide household tasks. A wise older woman said, "Whatever you learn to do when young comes easy to you all your life."

Be Efficient

"She senses that her gain is good, her lamp does not go out at night. She stretches out her hands to the distaff, and her hands grasp the spindle" (Prov. 31:18-19).

The ideal woman carefully evaluates what she is doing, and decides whether the results justify the work involved. She values her time. Once she's decided on a project, she becomes involved in what she's doing, and keeps at it. She doesn't quit at the first opportunity.

The ideal wife still works with her hands at household tasks, even though she's attained some success as a businesswoman. She's not preoccupied with self-decoration or with merely fashionable accomplishments.

"She is not afraid of the snow for her household, for all her household are clothed with scarlet. She makes coverings for herself; her clothing is fine linen and purple" (Prov. 31:21-22). This woman who manages everything well plans for winter. She saves ahead, provides clothing necessary for the future. She also dresses well herself, in the finest she can afford, as a woman of dignity and power. Any husband wants his wife to look her best, and children want to feel proud of their mother. However hard and capably she works, she's not to look like a drudge! The Bible says clothes are important—they're not to be overdone, or underdone. (See 1 Tim. 2:9-10; 1 Peter 3:3-4; Isa. 64:6; Rev. 19:8.)

Be Prudent

"She makes linen garments and sells them, and supplies belts to the tradesmen" (Prov. 31:24). Amazing. This remarkable woman now finds that she has time to start a manufacturing business of her own. Traders were always moving through Israel by camel caravan going from Egypt to Damascus and beyond. This wife learned to produce something that was in demand. She could sell it locally, or to merchants traveling to faraway places. Her ability was valued in the marketplace.

Sometimes wives who make no effort to compete in the marketplace resent their husbands' long hours away from home. They imagine all those hours in pleasant surroundings, perhaps among well-dressed secretaries, to be hours of pleasure and relaxation. Therefore, they reason, husbands should devote their evenings and weekends to making life pleasant for the poor wives who have to stay at home all the time.

A little experience for the wife in meeting the demands of a boss, or standards required for a sale, could help a marriage. It might make her more sympathetic with the stress and strain her husband undergoes to earn a living. It could help her to appreciate the privilege and freedom of staying at home.

Be Diligent

"She looks well to the ways of her household, and does not eat the bread of idleness" (Prov. 31:27). We've already been told that. Why again? Because this lady and her husband are now magnates in the town. People might think she's above tending to little household affairs. But the Bible makes clear that no one is ever above working with his hands. Some societies have made *not* working with the hands a matter of status. To us, working with the hands is part of our democratic ideal. A great man will boast that he built his own rock garden, or made a cabinet in his basement, or repaired his car with his own hands. A woman senator boasted that she could make a chocolate cake.

Reach to the Needy

"She extends her hand to the poor; and she stretches out her hands to the needy" (Prov. 31:20). Our ideal woman now excels as wife, as household manager, and as businesswoman. But that is not enough—we're to lay down our lives for others, as our Lord laid down His life for us. "Bear one another's burdens, and thus fulfill the law of Christ" (Gal. 6:2). All around us we see the have-nots, the poor, the deprived. Jesus said, "To the extent that you did it to one of these brothers of Mine, even the least of them; you did it to Me. . . . You did not do it to one of the least of these, you did not do it to Me" (Matt. 25:40, 45).

Harriet keeps house and power-sews upholstery in an automobile plant. She often stops at nursing homes on her way home from work. "I just love old people," she says, "and some of those people are so lonely, no one ever comes to see them. I can't give them much, but I can take them the love of Christ."

Marlene teaches part-time, works on a Ph.D. degree, graces political occasions for her lawyer-husband, entertains, and cares for her two children. She looks after a large house with the help of a high school girl. She also helped a Vietnamese family of five to get settled in this country by having them in her home for six weeks. Says Marlene, "They were marvelous. It was no problem. They helped, they fitted in. We really enjoyed having them."

Even a working mother needs to allocate some of her time and proceeds to needs beyond those of herself and family. If it seems impossible, perhaps she can cut down her working hours, or get more help from her family. One of the chief joys of earning is the joy of giving. (See Eph. 4:28; James 1:27; Acts 20:35.)

Set Priorities

This ideal woman in Proverbs seems to have found time, energy, and ability for everything. We lesser mortals, however, have to do some negotiating with our families. Sometimes we have to make choices. Where father and mother both work, and children at home still need care, it takes some doing to hold everything together.

As you put God first in your home, you gain perspective. You can help each other sort out the important from the unimportant as you listen to each other.

Not long after we were married, my husband found me up on a ladder washing woodwork. "What are you doing that for?" he asked. "It doesn't show where you've washed and where you haven't." I looked, and sure enough it didn't. I came down off the ladder and waited till it did show before I washed the woodwork.

Hans and Deborah both teach, both share equally in housework and child care. She cooks, unless she's too busy. Then he takes over. He shops, because he likes to. They share the cleaning and laundry. When he was completing his Ph.D. thesis along with teaching, she did everything.

When she was four months pregnant, she took 15 students on a three-week seminar course to France. She came back exhausted, and for a few weeks did nothing but teach her classes and rest in bed. He carried all the home responsibilities. Their boy of nine takes care of the yard, sets the table, and does dishes. The Bible gives a clue for working out such difficult adjustments: "Give preference to one another in honor" (Rom. 12:10).

Other couples work it out in other ways. If the wife must work for financial reasons, it seems only fair to divide the housework and child care down the middle. As children get older, they will benefit from taking on responsibilities.

I always wanted my husband to give his all to the church. Yet I wanted time of my own to study, to teach, to do some writing. I told him to spend what little time he had at home with the children. We hired the housework and handyman jobs done long before some would have felt we could afford it. No superwoman in strength, I had to learn to trust the Lord for the household help I needed. God always miraculously provided.

I believe the Bible makes very clear that a woman who gets married must carry ultimate responsibility for her own home and children. She can't look to the government or someone else to provide for her children so she can pursue a career unhindered.

Of course, any woman has a perfect *right* to pursue a career unencumbered. She need not get married. If she resents the responsibilities inherent in marriage, why marry to make some man's life miserable? Leave the man for some woman who would appreciate him. And why bring children into the world if she doesn't want to look after them? No one, not even our society, demands that every woman marry and bear children.

But if she has already given birth to children, she's locked in. She's committed not only to loving her children, but to caring for them as long as they need her.

Be Rewarded

And what, if any, is the reward for all this diligence? "Her children rise up and bless her; her husband also, and he praises her, saying: 'Many daughters have done nobly, but you excel them all'" (Prov. 31:28-29).

A wife and mother is repaid in love and appreciation for all she has given to those she loved. This is why mothering can be the most selfish thing in the world—you get so much back. As the wife has grown, the husband has also grown, and so has their marriage. He speaks of her in the hyperbole of love. "Give her the product of her hands, and let her works praise her in the gates" (Prov.

31:31). Isn't that what a woman desires? To be valued for what she can do, not as a sex object, not as a status symbol or possession for her husband, but as a person in her own right? In public places—"the gates"—as well as in the family, this woman is recognized as a person who has accomplished things. She benefits richly from what she has invested in others.

5
How to Make Used Goods Better Than New

A bride calls the church to arrange for her wedding. The secretary asks for names of bride and groom, their addresses and phone numbers. The addresses turn out to be the same.

The minister suffers a mild tremor, about two on the Richter earthquake scale, when he notes the addresses. The couple come in to talk to him. He decides since they're already living together, they'd probably be better off married. He talks to them about accepting Christ as Saviour, and establishing their home on a Christian basis.

A young woman attending a group for singles comes in to talk with the pastor. She's been married and divorced, has lived with one man and then another since her divorce. Now she's decided to become a Christian and get her life "straightened out."

On many different levels of commitment, couples live together today without getting married. Of total households in the United States, a significant minority consist of couples cohabiting, but not married. Is there any place for them in the Christian community? How do they fit in?

A Woman of Sychar

On a day in the early part of Jesus' ministry, a woman who lived in the village of Sychar took her jar to the well to get water.

Women ordinarily went to the village source of water in the

53

morning or evening, when it was cool. But this woman went "the sixth hour," or at noon. Probably she wanted to escape the cold looks of the townswomen. They may have viewed her as an indecent woman, for she was living with a man out of wedlock.

No doubt she despised herself. Five different men had married her. And five different men either died or found something wrong with her. According to Moses' law, divorce was allowed—because of the hardness of the human hearts (Matt. 19:8). Moses didn't institute divorce. He simply regulated a practice already in existence.

The ancient law was stated in Deuteronomy: "When a man takes a wife and marries her, and it happens that she finds no favor in his eyes because he has found some indecency in her, and he writes her a certificate of divorce and puts it in her hand and sends her out from his house, and she leaves his house, and goes and becomes another man's wife . . ." (Deut. 24:1-2).

Only a man could initiate divorce. The woman had no rights whatsoever. She could not even compel the man to give her a bill of divorcement, permitting her to remarry.

The regulation from Deuteronomy was variously interpreted strictly or loosely. Among the Jews, just before the time of Christ, the school of Shammah took a strict view. Only some action contrary to the rules of virtue, like adultery, justified divorce. But Shammah's disciple Hillel taught the opposite view. He said, "some uncleanness" could mean anything that displeased the husband, like too much salt in his food, or finding someone he liked better. So men took their choice of which school they wanted to follow.

No doubt similar differences of interpretation existed among the Samaritans. The woman of Sychar followed the Samaritan religion which accepted only the Pentateuchal books of the Old Testament—Genesis, Exodus, Leviticus, Numbers, and Deuteronomy. Those included the law on divorce.

I imagine the woman showed what she had been through—in her face, now hard and empty; in her figure, now drooping with middle-aged weariness. She may have been suffering torments of rejection by all those husbands, and also tortures of resentment against them. Maybe her last husband had even refused her a bill of divorcement. She needed that to be able to marry again. And perhaps she didn't have the strength left to survive in her society without a man. A woman was under the control of her nearest male relative, whether father, husband, brother, or son. Her husbands could have divorced her because she bore them no children.

And now, because of her lifestyle, even the women rejected her. She was one of life's losers. She came to the well when she thought no one would be there. She didn't want old wounds reopened.

As she approached, she saw a man sitting on the curb of the well. Who was he? How did he happen to be at a well? Only women drew water, unless it was for sheep. He obviously had no flock. He looked like a rabbi or teacher, dressed in the long white robe of that profession.

A Thirsty Man

"When therefore the Lord knew that the Pharisees had heard that Jesus was making and baptizing more disciples than John (although Jesus Himself was not baptizing, but His disciples were), He left Judea, and departed again into Galilee" (John 4:1-3).

Jesus Himself had been baptized by John at the Jordan. Then He spent 40 days on the Mountain of Temptation. After that He went back to minister with John at the Jordan. But Jesus was proving to be an even more popular religious leader than John. The Pharisees of Jerusalem were jealous. They had always been the religious elite, and wanted to hold their position.

So Jesus quietly withdrew from the territory of religious privilege, Judea. He headed north toward motley Galilee. For this journey Jews normally traveled up the Jordan Valley or detoured through Perea to the east of the Jordan. At considerable inconvenience they avoided going through Samaria.

"And He had to pass through Samaria" (John 4:4). Why? Did Jesus foresee one wretched woman at a well? Did His move foreshadow the universality of His message? It was not to be confined to Jews, nor to the religiously privileged. It was to be offered to the whole world—including losers. Jesus had a heart for those who couldn't make their lives come together. He reached out to a type of person not always welcomed in our churches.

In going through Samaria, Jesus showed that He was a person not bound by convention. He broke the usual pattern.

"He came to a city of Samaria, called Sychar, near the parcel of ground that Jacob gave to his son Joseph; and Jacob's well was there. Jesus therefore, being wearied from His journey, was sitting thus by the well" (John 4:5-6).

Jesus and His disciples had grown tired climbing up from the Jordan. Round and round they walked, first through the hills of the arid wilderness, then up and down among the mountains of the central range. They passed hillsides covered with vineyards and olive groves.

At last Jesus and the disciples reached Jacob's well, at the foot of Mount Ebal. You can visit the well today, and sit on the edge of the well. You can look out over the same broad valley of grainfields below.

Jesus saw a lone woman coming down the hill with a water jug on her head. Anyone but Jesus would have drawn back and ignored her. Barriers of race, religion, sex, character, and social position should have separated Him from her. No rabbi would ever hold conversation with a woman alone in public, not even his wife or mother. Surely not a strange woman. Certainly not a woman of questionable character.

Yet Jesus saw the woman's enormous need, her enormous potential. He tactfully opened the conversation by asking her to do something for Him. In so doing, He showed one way that we can bridge a gulf between ourselves and another person.

"Give Me a drink" (John 4:7). The woman was all too aware of her needs, her inferiority. Jesus expressed a need of His own, one she could easily fill. We don't reach people without Christ by acting like superior beings who confer benefits. We establish a relationship by sharing, by accepting as well as giving.

Our neighbors who don't know Christ may be able to instruct us in gardening, or in laying down stones for a patio. We can benefit from their knowledge and they from ours. Everyone we meet knows more than we do about something. As we find out about another's area of knowledge, we learn. As we open ourselves to instruction or help, we may also open up the other person to letting us share Christ.

In asking for that drink of water, Jesus understood that all of us need to be needed. We want someone to ask us to sing, to serve on a committee, to speak, to bake our special dish, to write out a recipe, or to join a group. We love to be asked for advice. We enjoy having someone request a small favor that comes easily to us, but that means a lot to him.

No one else in that town would have asked such a woman for a personal favor. But Jesus did, and she expressed amazement. She recognized Him as a Jew by His dress and His accent. Vacationing in Alabama, we met a girl from Michigan, our home state. "It's nice to talk to someone without an accent," she said. We spoke briefly with a couple of young men camping in a state park. "Wheah yo-all from?" one of them asked. "Yo-all have an accent." Jesus wasn't worried about His accent.

Samaritan Religion

The woman also realized that He was a person of far different social position from herself. She felt rebuked by His very presence. Yet she was pleased, flattered, surprised that He asked something of her. "How is it that You, being a Jew, ask me for a drink since I am a Samaritan woman?" (John 4:9)

A deep hatred separated Jews from Samaritans. If you visit Nablus today, on the north slope of Mt. Ebal, you can find what remains of the ancient Samaritans. Samaritan priests will show you a much-revered scroll of the Pentateuch. They'll tell you that about 200 Samaritans still exist, still go through their ancient ritual of animal sacrifice on Mt. Gerizim, just south of Ebal. They focus on Passover, in the spring, as a great celebration and get-together. Samaritans who have intermarried or left the community come back for that.

The Jews of Jesus' time regarded Samaritans as a rival sect. In 721 B.C., Assyria carried away the leading citizens of the northern 10 tribes, leaving only the poorest people to cultivate the land. Then the Assyrians brought in others to repopulate the country.

These intermarried with Jews, and worked out a mongrel kind of religion.

Two centuries later, when the Jews returned from captivity to rebuild the temple in Jerusalem, Samaritans offered to help. But the Jews, regarding them as inferiors, refused. The Samaritans became indignant, and set up a rival temple on Mt. Gerizim. During the five centuries that followed, the rift deepened. By the time of Christ, the Jews had "no dealings with Samaritans" (John 4:9).

Thirst

In talking with the woman, Jesus quickly moved the conversation from His physical thirst of the moment to her need for eternity. "If you knew the gift of God, and who it is who says to you, 'Give Me a drink,' you would have asked Him, and He would have given you Living Water" (John 4:10).

That woman of Sychar was not entirely sure what He was talking about, but she felt eager to continue the conversation. She said, "Sir, You have nothing to draw with and the well is deep; where then do You get that Living Water?" (John 4:11)

Jacob had dug that well long ago for his sheepherders. It was inherited by the family of Jacob's son Joseph when they brought Joseph's bones back from Egypt. Once the well had been 100 feet deep. Today it is only 78 feet deep, but you can still let down a bucket into its depths and drink from its pure fresh water, as Jesus did.

"You are not greater than our father Jacob . . . who gave us the well, and drank of it himself, and his sons, and his cattle?" (John 4:12) She wondered—could this Man provide a bubbling stream in this area, where Jacob could find none? Could He get water somehow into her house, so she wouldn't have to make this wearisome trip to the well every day?

Jesus answered, "Everyone who drinks of this water shall thirst again; but whoever drinks of the water that I shall give him shall never thirst; but the water that I shall give him shall become in him a well of water springing up to eternal life" (John 4:13-14).

Whatever He was talking about, she wanted it. Perhaps in that moment Jesus opened up to her a glimpse of spiritual possibilities. Something wonderful inside herself to quench her agonizing thirst. Certainly she wanted life beyond what she'd known. "Sir, give me this water, so I will not be thirsty, nor come all the way here to draw" (John 4:15).

The woman would gladly have added to her life whatever Jesus was offering. Lots of people today would like to add Jesus to their lives, but don't want to change. He knows we all need to repent. If we add something new to our household, like a new refrigerator, or new drapes, or a new dining room set, we have to clear out the old before moving in the new. Jesus knew the woman needed to change her present life. He wanted to reach her conscience. So He said, "Go, call your husband, and come here" (John 4:16). He thereby put His finger on the very sore spot.

Perhaps she blushed as she said, "I have no husband" (John 4:17). Jesus made no judgment, offered no word of advice. He only enlarged upon what she had stated. "You have well said, 'I have no husband'; for you have had five husbands; and the one whom you now have is not your husband; this you have said truly" (John 4:17-18).

Jesus simply verified that the woman was telling the truth. Yet He tore her mask away, as He tears all our masks away. We stand before Him with every secret plainly visible.

"I perceive that You are a prophet" (John 4:19). At first she had seen Him as "a Jew" (John 4:9). Then she saw Him as "greater than our father Jacob" (John 4:12). Now she saw Him as "a prophet"—one who speaks for God (John 4:19).

As she saw her own sin, she asked an important question. Where was the place to present a sin offering? "Our fathers worshiped in this mountain; and you people say that in Jerusalem is the place where men ought to worship" (John 4:20).

Perhaps the woman wanted to divert Him from the subject of her sin by getting into a theological discussion. It's been done many times since. She knew her religion well. She also had mastered the differences between Jewish and Samaritan beliefs.

Jesus replied that the hour had come when it didn't matter whether people worshiped on Mt. Gerizim or at Jerusalem. He said salvation was of the Jews, and that the whole Old Testament stood, not just the Pentateuch. He then declared to this drained woman a central truth about God, which He had declared to no one else. "An hour is coming, and now is, when the true worshipers shall worship the Father in spirit and truth; for such people the Father seeks to be His worshipers. God is Spirit; and those who worship Him must worship in spirit and truth" (John 4:23-24).

A tremendous truth. A person is body, soul, and spirit. The physical body can be ministered to with physical things, like water. The place of worship can matter to the soul, which is the part of personality with roots in one historical tradition or another. But since God is Spirit, only the spirit can connect with His. He seeks those who understand this, for they alone can reach out to Him in true worship.

The woman knew from the Pentateuch that a Messiah was promised. The Jews had a much fuller expectation of the Messiah. But she knew the words of Moses: "The Lord your God will raise up for you a Prophet like me from among you, from your countrymen, you shall listen to Him" (Deut. 18:15).

To this disreputable woman Jesus made His supreme announcement: "I who speak to you am He" (John 4:26).

A Witness in Sychar

The conversation ended when the disciples returned with the food they'd bought. They were amazed to find Jesus talking with a woman. But they had learned not to question His departures from convention. As we look closely at Scripture, we find a lot of things at variance with practices that have become conventional to us. We need to keep expecting the new and different from Jesus. We need to beware of equating what is only conventional with what is truly Christ's way.

The woman became so excited about Jesus that she forgot what she had come to the well for. It would be as if you or I met Jesus in the supermarket, and became so excited we walked off without the groceries we'd come to buy. Or met Him in the library and left our books sitting there. She forgot her physical thirst in having found satisfaction for her spiritual thirst, "and went into the city, and said to the men, 'Come, see a Man who told me all things that I have done; this is not the Christ, is it?'" (John 4:28-29) The woman of Sychar came to a full realization of who this remarkable Man was. . . . more than a Jew, more than a great man, more than a prophet.

While the woman was gone, the disciples in loving concern urged Jesus to eat. He said, "I have food to eat that you do not know about" (John 4:32). They were mystified, wondering if someone else had brought Him food. Jesus explained that some things in life are more important even than eating. "My food is to do the will of Him who sent Me, and to accomplish His work" (John 4:34).

Sitting on that well, looking out over the fertile valley, Jesus said it would be four months until the now-green grain would be ready for harvesting. In Israel, grain grows during the winter, rainy season, and is harvested about April.

Jesus then looked toward Sychar, and saw the townsfolk coming down Mt. Ebal towards Him. In their wheat-colored clothing, they looked like ripened grain. The disciples were to turn away from the unripe grain in the fields—representing the physical bread they had offered Him—and look at that ripe harvest of souls ready to be reaped. He had sown the seed; the disciples could now reap the harvest. Then they would all rejoice together, as sower and reapers.

When the people of Sychar came to Jesus and heard Him speak, they asked Him to stay, and "He stayed there two days. And many more believed because of His Word; and they were saying to the woman, 'It is no longer because of what you said that we believe, for we have heard for ourselves and know that this One is indeed the Saviour of the world'" (John 4:40-42).

The woman of Sychar didn't detain them in town telling them about her experience. She directed them to Jesus. Then they took the initiative, and asked Him to stay. During the two days that Jesus was with them, they came to understand that He was even more than a Jewish—or Samaritan—Messiah. He was the *"Saviour of the world."*

A Changed Woman

How did the woman's life turn out? We don't know. Jesus didn't condemn her, didn't judge her, He just brought her to Himself. He left it to the power of God in her life to straighten out that life.

We need to be careful not to drive people away from Jesus by judging them by our standards, or even by biblical standards, right as those are. We need, first of all, to bring a person to Jesus. We all come to Him on the same level—just as we are. He'll take care of what needs to be changed in us.

Through this woman with a really messed-up life, Jesus reached a whole community. Her witness laid the groundwork for Philip's later great success in that same region (Acts 8:4-8).

How do you treat a cohabiting unmarried man and woman who visit your church on a Sunday morning? Do you make it clear you do not approve of their lifestyle? Do you ignore them, or view them coldly, because they make you feel uncomfortable?

Jesus accepted the Samaritan woman as a person whose life He could change.

6
How to Use Your Power to Choose

Today, women face many pressures that urge them out of the home. The traditional nuclear family with father working, mother at home, constitutes fewer than 10 percent of all American households.

Yet many women still find life at home challenging. Certainly, they enjoy more options than any woman tied to full-time employment.

Says Donna, "I feel a woman in the home has more power in the world today than any other person. I have impact on so many lives. My children talk over their problems with me, and they listen to me. My husband listens to me.

"I started out marriage well on my way in a career as a buyer for a chain of retail stores. Trained by the former business manager for Adrienne, the fashion designer, I had quite a future in business.

"My mother hadn't urged motherhood, since she favored a career. At most I thought of having two children. In giving me six children, I feel God chose for me a finer thing than anything I ever hoped for. Motherhood is a big thing with me."

A Woman at Home
To many, being a woman in the home is still the ideal. Why? Many women grew up in that kind of home. The biblical account of the

human race starts out with a man, a woman, and their children. When Christ came to earth, God placed Him in a home where the man worked as a carpenter, the woman cared for the home and children.

Many American women supported by their husbands live like queens. Others value being at home with their children enough to sacrifice material goods for that privilege.

Betty, like Donna, loves being the wife at home. "I feel sorry for wives who must go out to work for financial reasons. I would rather live in a smaller house, on a more modest scale in order to have time to spend at home, with my children. I feel especially sorry for wives driven by an inner compulsion to escape the home. I think they miss some of the best of family life."

Says Elaine, another stay-at-home wife, "I hope to make my home a place my husband and children would rather be than somewhere else. A woman at home has time and opportunity to create a loving atmosphere of restfulness and security, one conducive to growth. A haven. My husband, a professional man, faces constant stress in his work. He lives a high-pressure life. When I worked, I wasn't free to focus on him. I like having time to talk over his challenges, meet his needs. I have time to teach my children values, time to learn about their personalities, to study their needs and problems."

Woman

What is woman? Why should she take it upon herself to meet a man's needs? Throughout history, and in many parts of the world today, woman is chattel, plaything, or servant. In Western society, woman has benefited from the influence of Christianity. She's a person. Yet all too often she's a rebel. What did God intend her to be? What can she be?

The woman at home, free from the responsibility of earning a living, has freedom to choose. How shall she spend her time? Which potentials in herself shall she develop? What personal, family, and societal values shall she claim as her own to pursue?

Before God created man, He prepared the universe. When all was ready, He said, "Let Us make man in Our image, according to

Our likeness. . . . And God created man in His own image, in the image of God created him; male and female He created them" (Gen. 1:26-27).

In the ideal home, man and woman are one, neither ruling over the other. "He blessed them, and named them Man, in the day when they were created" (Gen. 5:2).

God told them both to be fruitful, both to have dominion. "And God blessed them; and God said to them, 'Be fruitful and multiply, and fill the earth, and subdue it; and rule over the fish of the sea and over the birds of the sky, and over every living thing that moves on the earth. . . . I have given you every plant . . . food for you'" (Gen. 1:28-29).

So woman and man were given the same kind of body, soul, and spirit. Each possessed a body formed of elements already in existence in the universe. "Then the Lord God formed man of dust from the ground" (Gen. 2:7). After God had formed woman out of man's rib, Adam said, "This is now bone of my bones, and flesh of my flesh; she shall be called Woman, because she was taken out of Man" (Gen. 2:23).

Each possessed a soul. Each as a personality was capable of exercising dominion. Women, like men, can learn physics, develop hybrid corn or roses, drive cars, oversee factories, raise cattle or chickens.

Pet lovers insist that animals also have a soul. We share with animals the gift of sentient life. The Hebrew Bible uses the word *nephesh*, "a breathing creature," for animals as well as men. Each individual—animal or human, male or female—has its own personality—a set of emotions, a distinctive pattern of behavior, a self-conscious life.

But, men and women have something more than do the animals—a spirit that can reach out for God. A tree has a body, but no soul or spirit. An animal possesses a body and a soul. Man alone has body, soul, and spirit, and can relate to the eternal God.

How is woman, equipped with body, soul, and spirit, to use her God-given abilities?

Some women express creativity through their environment. They paint, paper, sew, refinish furniture, and put furnishings together artistically. They raise flowers and plants, study flower arranging. Most women have available the elements for creating a beautiful environment.

For that first man and woman, God set up what He considered the perfect environment. "And the Lord God planted a garden toward the east in Eden; and there He placed the man whom He had formed" (Gen. 2:8).

That garden offered beauty—"every tree that is pleasing to the sight" (Gen. 2:9). A woman created in the image of God wants to make her home as beautiful as possible. One of the most beautiful homes I ever saw was that of a missionary in Bangkok, Thailand. It was furnished in "early missionary" furniture—cumbersome hand-me-downs. Yet it was a fairyland of loveliness. Plants grew up from the floor, hung down over the window openings like draperies. Plants decorated the tables and desks. Beauty of surroundings doesn't necessarily mean a fine house in suburbia, or a place in the country. Anyone who loves beauty can create it with very little.

Other women express their creativity through food preparation. God provided something to eat for Adam and Eve—"every tree . . . and good for food" (Gen. 2:9). If we want our families to find home an attractive place, we have to provide good meals. A well-stocked refrigerator and full cupboards definitely add appeal. One time our daughter stopped at our house when Bart and I were on vacation. "But I didn't stay very long," she said. "There wasn't anything to eat in the house."

Many women enjoy cooking and food preparation. Some make a great art of cooking. Others study the science of nutrition to give their families optimum health through diet.

Personal Growth

Women at home have special opportunities to develop spiritually. God knew that as a spiritual being, man needed more than beauty and food. In that first home grew "the tree of life also in the midst of the garden" (Gen. 2:9). Originally, man was free to eat of it. God wanted man to enter fully into His own life of the spirit.

Says Elaine, "For a woman at home, there's so much time to

think, so many opportunities for spiritual growth. You can be filling the mind with all kinds of good things—learning Scripture, listening to tapes, hearing messages on the radio, going to Bible classes. Praying. All day long. While you work."

Donna says, "I have to keep in good shape spiritually because I affect the whole family. If I come apart, family life is a disaster."

The woman at home has special opportunities to do for others. "A river flowed out of Eden . . . and from there it divided" (Gen. 2:10). Blessing for others flowed from that ideal home. Through and out of the garden flowed the great Tigris and Euphrates Rivers, in addition to several other temporary channels in that great flood plain. Archeology concurs that life began somewhere in that general region east of the Mediterranean.

Jesus spoke of water as both physical and spiritual. "If any man is thirsty, let him come to Me and drink. He who believes in Me, as the Scripture said, 'From his innermost being shall flow rivers of living water'" (John 7:37-38). Every home needs both physical and spiritual water. Life-giving water nourished the Garden. It also flowed out to bless other regions. Service, hospitality, loving, and caring must flow out, or the home will stagnate.

The woman at home can express her own creativity as she serves other people. She forms the backbone of many volunteer efforts. The value of work does not equal the amount of money paid for it.

Says Elaine, "Being a woman at home, I can reach out to other women at home. We have a Bible study for young mothers on our block. We help each other. And I try to make my home a place where my children will bring their friends."

A doctor's wife volunteers to organize church dinners for 500 people. "I like to do this. It really challenges me."

One wife spent six months learning to write braille so she could transcribe textbooks for blind people.

Another wife studied Christian education and became an expert Sunday School superintendent. A friend of mine makes her Christian witness felt as a member of a school board.

God provided work in that ideal garden home. And many women at home find creativity in their work—gardening, cleaning, maintaining the home. "Then the Lord God took the man and put him into the Garden of Eden to cultivate it and keep it" (Gen. 2:15). We all need work.

Says Betty, "I can't say that I really enjoy cleaning house. But I enjoy a clean house. And I can see the immediate results of my work. Not everyone holding a job can see instant results. And I'm my own boss. I can be creative, get to all the rooms and closets, knit, sew, take care of pets, and raise plants. I can help the neighbors, serve a super meal for my husband. I can be as busy as I want. Satisfaction comes from doing a good job, from knowing that my family needs me."

One wife studied construction and with her husband's assistance added a bedroom and family room to their house. Another learned how to do all kinds of home repairs, including plumbing and electrical installation.

Keeping a home involves work. Any mother of small children knows she can reduce her house to chaos by simply relaxing for a day. Children at any age left to themselves will spin off into all kinds of mischief or danger. Husbands untended may forget to come home.

My mother used to say, "I regard what I do at home as my job. Everybody has to contribute something to the world's work. This is what I do."

Free Will

The woman at home enjoys considerable freedom. In that ideal home, God gave ample liberty. No one enjoys a lot of restrictions. Adam and Eve had only one. They could eat of any tree in that whole garden, except one (Gen. 2:16-17). Certain plants grow in the world today that we ought to steer clear of, for our own good. Some prove instantly poisonous; others destroy slowly and insidiously.

Adam and Eve needed that simple test of obedience. How else could man develop his moral nature? How else could fellowship with his Creator mean anything, if no alternative existed? God gave man a free will, and a test on which to exercise that will. Just as He gave work for exercising the body, and animals to name for exercising the mind.

Woman was put in that garden as co-partner with man. But she was also counterpart and complement. Adam enjoyed the garden, and became acquainted with all the animals and birds in it. But he was still lonely. God said, "It is not good for the man to be alone; I will make him a helper suitable for him" (Gen. 2:18). So God presented something more for Adam's delight—Woman.

Many a young man has suddenly wakened to the girl next door, or the one in chemistry lab, seeing her for the first time as Woman. He wants her to share his home, grace it, enliven it, make life worth living. Adam saw the woman as someone he needed, part of himself, one who could fill in the empty places. " 'This is now bone of my bones, and flesh of my flesh; she shall be called Woman, because she was taken out of Man.' For this cause a man shall leave his father and his mother, and shall cleave to his wife; and they shall become one flesh" (Gen. 2:23-24).

Elaine enjoys the role of studying and meeting her husband's needs. Every woman has to, if she wants her marriage to grow and blossom—or even hold together.

Peggy married Tom, a very conscientious young man, of high moral character. She felt she need never fear that Tom would divorce her. But she didn't want her marriage to consist of loyalty based on duty. She immediately set out to study her husband's needs and made a business of filling those needs. Tom found himself well nourished in every way—emotionally, physically, intellectually, spiritually. He found it easy to respond to Peggy's needs, no matter what the outside pressures. So Peggy was equally well nourished, and their relationship grew with the years.

Everybody has empty places—weaknesses, shortcomings, peculiarities, immaturities—as well as individual strengths and potentialities for glorious soaring. A wife's commitment as helper, to fill in those empty places, isn't all give and no take. While we all know of bitter exceptions, people generally tend to get back what they give. Other people's attitudes toward us tend to be a mirror image of our attitudes toward them. "Give, and it will be given to you" (Luke 6:38).

A marriage equals only the sum of what two people put into it. If each plans on taking all he can get, giving as little as he can get by with, the emotional bank account will soon go into the red. The marriage will sooner or later go out of business. Each must work at adding to the emotional bank account.

Temptations

The woman at home lives in a seemingly protected environment. Yet she faces special temptations. She must choose whether or not to succumb.

Eve shared Adam's perfect environment. They enjoyed total communication with God, and with each other. No barriers. But their home, like even the most perfect marriage today, also presented temptation. There was someone else in that garden. The Bible indicates that he is still busy getting into homes. We're warned, "Be of sober spirit, be on the alert. Your adversary, the devil, prowls about like a roaring lion, seeking someone to devour" (1 Peter 5:8). To Eve this adversary appeared as *nachash,* a shining one. To every modern Eve he presents the age-old temptations, changed only in their appearance.

Audrey regards too much daytime television as destructive of spiritual life and values. "Those soap operas make it seem as though everybody is going to bed with someone else's husband or wife—as though there's nothing unusual about a wife not knowing who the father of her baby is."

Betty says, "I think the very freedom that I enjoy can be a temptation. If I'm disorganized I don't get enough done. I can easily fritter away a whole day watching television, or idly reading. I can slack off on the job, serve the minimum for meals, let my standards go down. Or overeat." We'll all agree that a dirty house or a sloppy and overfed wife would put a strain on any marriage.

Elaine sees temptations even more insidious. "At home, with all the opportunities to grow, it's easy to find yourself feeling superior to your husband spiritually, looking down on him, feeling critical of him. Also, it's easy to let negative feelings multiply. As moods swing up and down, you can all too easily stay on the down side. You tend to forget all you have to be grateful for, to want more, more, more.

"And if your husband is like a lot of men, he may have entered marriage not realizing he had to work at it. He works long hours, but doesn't realize you have needs. Being at home, you may become more aware of your needs than if you were working. If another man shows you a little attention—a neighbor, a friend, even someone in a couples' Bible study—you may be in trouble."

Eve listened to the shining one. "Satan disguises himself as an angel of light" (2 Cor. 11:14). First he taunted her with her circumscribed life, made her restriction seem unjust. Satan pointed out the one thing God had warned Eve not to do. "Indeed, has God said, 'You shall not eat from any tree of the garden'?" (Gen. 3:1)

Eve lingered to discuss the matter. Anyone who hangs around arguing with Satan is sure to get bested. The safest thing is to flee the temptation immediately. "Resist the devil and he will flee from you" (James 4:7). "Flee . . . youthful lusts" (2 Tim. 2:22).

"But," says Elaine, "you don't always have the strength at the time to deny the attraction, to just swallow your emotions. The looks and the words feed you where you're starved. I found myself obsessed with thinking about a man in our Bible study. I thought I could handle it, but I couldn't. He kept feeding the attraction with his looks, his words.

"I went to a pastor, and he recommended a marriage counselor who helped me express my needs to my husband. My husband was at first furious, then hurt. But he recognized where he had left me open to such an attraction. We began to be more open to each other about our needs. Now we spend more time talking than we did previously.

"The other man has moved away now, and I put him out of my mind. But recently when I saw him again briefly, there was the old attraction. The best thing to do is to stay away from such a person. Sometimes, however, as in the case of a neighbor or co-worker, this is not possible.

"However, there are constant choices to be made. A person can identify those things which feed the feelings and deepen the relationship. You can avoid being alone together, talking on the telephone, conversing on a personal level. These actions can be identified and stopped through an act of the will made possible through prayer. We do not have perfect control over our thoughts and feelings, but we do have control over how we act as a result of our feelings.

"Through counseling, my basic problem has been identified as fantasizing, which was dismissed as school-girl crushes when I was growing up. It didn't even appear as a problem until after I was married and couldn't quit. I thank God that He loves me enough to forgive me for the fantasies I've had. I pray He'll help me bring 'every thought captive to the obedience of Christ'" (2 Cor. 10:5).

"When I look back on that particular temptation, I shudder when I think of what I might have destroyed had I said yes to my feelings. My husband and I are now rebuilding our marriage. It's much stronger than before."

Another wife suggests you can control your thoughts by following Paul's advice to fill up your mind with good things—all that's true, honest, pure, lovely (Phil. 4:8). Don't allow your mind to lie empty. It will sprout weeds.

Satan next tried to persuade Eve of the unreality of God's warning. "You surely shall not die!" (Gen. 3:4) Today Satan says, "You won't really destroy yourself, your family, your place in society, your self-respect, your pure and open relationship with God. Go ahead. Play around. Build up your ego a little. What harm in enjoying a little flattery? Indulge your passion. Why not? Everybody does it."

Satan next appealed to Eve's pride, as he appeals to the pride of every modern Eve. "Your eyes will be opened, and you will be like God, knowing good and evil" (Gen. 3:5).

Today, the world tells the woman at home that she's out of the mainstream of life, that she has buried herself in her family and lost her own identity. Sometimes the perpetual company of small children palls. Perhaps her husband doesn't talk to her enough. She misses any sense of sharing dominion in his corner of the world. Or he doesn't encourage her to develop her own God-given abilities. Anything or anyone who feeds her faltering ego constitutes a temptation.

The appeal to pride comes in different forms to different individuals. One woman wants a bigger house, a finer car, more clothes and house furnishings than she can afford. Another craves a job, a career, even too many church activities, whether these are right for her or not. Still another finds the flattering attention of another man extremely tempting.

"When the woman saw that the tree was good for food, and that it was a delight to the eyes, and that the tree was desirable to make one wise . . ." (Gen. 3:6). That first temptation hit Eve in the natural desires of the flesh. It also appealed to the lust of the eyes—she saw and wanted the beautiful fruit. In addition, it appealed to the pride of life. (See 1 John 2:15-17.) Satan cleverly launched a three-pronged attack on Eve's motivations.

Accountability

So "she took from its fruit and ate; and she gave also to her husband with her, and he ate" (Gen. 3:6). Innocence was gone. They had made their choice and would face the consequences.

Elaine, a modern Eve, with Christ in her heart, was able to surmount the temptation. She believed God's Word, that "the way of the treacherous is hard" (Prov. 13:15). She believed in God's standard for marriage.

God held the man accountable. Adam answered, "The woman whom Thou gavest to be with me, she gave me from the tree" (Gen. 3:12). He blamed the woman and God.

God also held the woman accountable, for a wife can't give her spiritual responsibility to her husband. Eve blamed the shining one. Modern man and woman blame their parents, the society around them, each other, their jobs or lack of jobs. Regardless of who is to blame, the consequences are the same. Paradise is lost. Man now needs suffering, sorrow, hard work, and hardship.

Sinful people couldn't handle all that leisure they had back in the Garden of Eden. So they were condemned to labor. "Cursed is the ground because of you; in toil you shall eat of it all the days of your life. Both thorns and thistles it shall grow for you" (Gen. 3:17-18). We constantly hit problems, snags, difficulties, and disappointments. We learn that thorns and thistles are brought forth for our own good.

Adam, not God, called the woman *Eve,* meaning "mother."

Many a woman doesn't want her husband calling her "Mother," suggesting responsibility, pain, sorrow, as well as joy. To her husband she wants to be Woman—lover, delight, companion, counterpart. A wife doesn't need another child. She wants her husband to be a source of strength.

Eve was caught in the desires, potential joys, suffering and sorrows of family life. "To the woman He said, 'I will greatly multiply your pain in childbirth, in pain you shall bring forth children; yet your desire shall be for your husband, and he shall rule over you'" (Gen. 3:16). The woman at home loves and needs her husband—sometimes more than he seems to need her.

As a mother, Eve suffered unspeakable anguish. She saw one of her sons murdered by the other. Yet she carried on, and bore another child. For with the condemnation, God also gave a prophecy and a promise. To the serpent He said, "I will put enmity between you and the woman, and between your seed and her seed; he shall bruise you on the head, and you shall bruise him on the heel" (Gen. 3:15).

History has recorded the age-long struggle between good and evil. Satan stands ready to hinder, hurt, tempt, spoil, and destroy.

Eve produced a godly line in Seth, from whom eventually came the Christ. In Christ's victory, Satan received a mortal wound. Only through Christ dwelling in us can we find day-to-day victory to overcome the wiles of the evil one.

The woman at home can create a paradise on earth. She can build into her home all the components God meant for man and woman together to enjoy. Or she can give way to the special temptations inherent in her style of life.

The woman at home can make an impact on her world as example, inspiration, leader, helper, comforter. She can be an influence through her husband and children, as well as through her own work. She can make her life count for God through the things she chooses to do, as well as through the things she chooses not to do.

7
How to Live with Complicated Relationships

"So many times I'd come home from work and find my husband's first wife in my home," said Wilma. Wilma lives with her second husband, Jim, her two children, and his two by a former marriage.

"Two years after we were married, Jim's first wife voluntarily signed over her children to us. At that time she said, 'I suppose I should totally remove myself from my children's lives.'"

Wilma went on to say, "Something inside of me—I think it was God—said, 'Wilma, you can't do that—you can't deprive those children of their mother.' So I left the door open for her to visit. I didn't realize at the time how hard it would be for me to cope with her presence—or that she would come so often. Due to my terrible sense of rejection from my first marriage, I felt threatened by her—even though she was married again. I couldn't forget that she was Wife One, while I was only Wife Two. I had a senseless fear of losing Jim. And she was always right there in the middle of our marriage.

"My husband who is pure goodness tried to reassure me that I had no reason to feel threatened. He had been emasculated and totally rejected by her before she left him. But he's so gentle and kind he wouldn't tell her not to visit the children. So I just suffered. The children would let her in while I was at work. I put up with it for the sake of my stepchildren. After all, at seven and nine, how could they cut off all relationship with their mother?"

Another wife, Betsey, for 10 years put up with her husband's infidelity in hopes of saving her home. "When the other woman first entered 11 years ago, I almost crumbled. Tom asked, 'What would you think about a divorce?' He spent a year making up his mind, and at that time decided not to divorce me. But he carried on with the other woman for the next 10 years. I thought I couldn't tell my parents, because they viewed Tom as a son. He'd simply say to me, 'I won't be home tonight.' If I confronted him with accusations, he'd get angry, then make me feel guilty, or stupid. He's very positive and strong. I learned not to start discussions in which I would only get hurt."

Many people in today's world live with unbelievably complicated relationships. A blended or reconstituted family may consist of his children, her children, and our children. A child may have two homes instead of one, and four sets of grandparents instead of two.

Leah, the plain older sister of beautiful Rachel, lived in an extremely difficult situation and survived. How did she do it? How did she function in her various relationships? We'll look at Leah as a person, as a wife, as a mother, as a sister, and as a daughter.

Leah as a Person

We first meet Leah when we learn that Laban had another daughter besides Rachel. "Now Laban had two daughters; the name of the older was Leah, and the name of the younger was Rachel" (Gen. 29:16). The account in Genesis describes the gorgeous Rachel, and how Jacob fell in love with her at first sight. He had traveled 400 miles on foot from Canaan, fleeing the wrath of his brother Esau after cheating him of the birthright. Jacob met Rachel at the well in Paddan-aram, where she came to water her father's flock of sheep. The sight of Rachel so excited Jacob that he immediately rolled away a great stone from the well's mouth. Ordinarily, that stone required all the shepherds to move it (Gen. 29:3). We conclude that Jacob was a very strong man, and also powerfully motivated. Probably Rachel was quite young at the time. Jacob willingly worked and waited seven years for her.

"Leah's eyes were weak, but Rachel was beautiful of form and face" (Gen. 29:17). Commentators have drawn various ideas out of the Hebrew word *rak,* used to describe Leah's eyes. The *King James Version* translates it as "tender eyed," and the *Living Bible* describes Leah as having "lovely eyes." But other versions translate the word to mean "dull-looking," "delicate," "weak," or "sore." It has even been suggested that Laban palmed off on Jacob a daughter whom he couldn't otherwise get rid of, because of her sore eyes.

Why this contrast in meanings? What does the word really mean? It's important to know, because this is the only adjective we have describing Leah. The Hebrew word *rak* comes from the root *rakak,* "to soften." The primary meaning of *rak* is "tender," literally or figuratively. Then by implication it can mean "weak." The *King James Version* translates *rak* a number of times as "tender"—tender grass, tender children, a tender calf, a tender and delicate woman, a tender man, a tender youth, tender mercies, tender grapes, a tender plant, a tender twig, a tender-hearted person. The *New American Standard Bible* translates the same word variously as "tender," "refined," "frail" (children), "inexperienced," "new" (grass), depending upon the context. The *New International Version* translates the same word as "tender," "gentle and sensitive," "new" (grass), "kindest" (acts), "blossoming" (vine), "in bloom," "tender or delicate."

So I think we're justified in thinking of Leah as having very lovely eyes, soft and expressive. The writer contrasts Leah's one beautiful feature with Rachel's many. Rachel was favored with beauty of both face and form (Gen. 29:17).

So we see poor Leah growing up under the shadow of a beautiful younger sister. A mother of two girls said to me, "People are so thoughtless. They are always remarking about how cute, clever, and remarkable our younger daughter is. The older daughter may be standing right there, and they don't say a word about her. She's quieter, not so vivid and sparkling. She feels it. Those remarks aren't good for her at all."

Leah was not as beautiful as her younger sister. Yet she had sensitive eyes—and probably wore her heart in her eyes.

Leah possessed the beautiful quality of humility—a priceless asset. Through her trials and blessings she learned to praise God. She was much more spiritual in nature than Rachel. It was Rachel, not Leah, who carried off her father's household gods—small idols of wood or stone—from Paddan-aram. The names Leah chose for her sons describe her spiritual pilgrimage. We see in four of those names her sense of closeness to God.

Yet Jacob favored the petulant and unspiritual Rachel. "God sees not as man sees, for man looks at the outward appearance, but the Lord looks at the heart" (1 Sam. 16:7). Leah showed enormous patience, love, and long-suffering toward Jacob. We might even wonder if Leah was really God's first choice for Jacob. It was Leah who gave birth to Judah, father of the tribe from which Christ came. And it was Leah who was finally buried with Jacob.

Leah as a Wife

The Genesis account tells how Jacob worked seven years for Rachel, "and they seemed to him but a few days because of his love for her" (Gen. 29:20).

Then came time for the wedding, which apparently only the men celebrated. "Now it came about in the evening that he [Laban] took his daughter Leah, and brought her to him; and Jacob went in to her" (Gen. 29:23). The bride's only part was to be led to the groom's tent in the evening, while heavily veiled. Jacob had similarly deceived his blind father when he stole Esau's birthright. So Jacob was only getting what he had given. "So it came about in the morning that, behold, it was Leah" (Gen. 29:25).

Why did Leah allow herself to be substituted for Rachel? Perhaps all those seven long years, she too had been in love with Jacob. Perhaps her father read this in her eyes. Perhaps she thought, *I'll be able to win his love, once I become his wife.* Afterward, she certainly did everything she could to please Jacob. She never berated him for loving her less than he loved Rachel. She tried pathetically to win his love.

Many wives since have gone to extraordinary lengths to

win or keep the love of husbands who denied their deepest loyalty.

Betsey put up with her husband's infidelity for 10 years in hopes of saving her home. "I did everything imaginable to please him. I gave up a little part-time job that I found enjoyable, because he said I needed to keep the house cleaner. He wanted me to quit all church activities—he felt threatened by a group I headed. On bad mornings I'd go out and clean the snow off his car. He would say I didn't clean it well enough. He would find things I hadn't done, but never praise anything I did. I developed a terrible self-image. His comments really destroyed me. If I had it to do over again, I don't think I'd try so hard to please him. I'd stand on my own feet more, be my own person."

Said Wilma, "I did everything imaginable to please my first husband. I'd shine his shoes, wait on him, abject myself before him to do anything he fancied. Nothing worked to save that marriage. I rode the bus to work, while he drove far out of his way to pick up a girl who worked at his office."

Leah apparently pleased Jacob to some degree. When he woke up in the morning and found it was Leah he'd married, he didn't refuse her. And he obviously didn't find her totally distasteful— her many children testify to that.

After the deception, Leah's father explained, "It is not the practice in our place, to marry the younger before the firstborn. Complete the bridal week of this one, and we will give you the other also for the service which you shall serve with me for another seven years" (Gen. 29:26-27).

In effect Laban said, "Go through the wedding festivities without a fuss, and at the end of the seven days' celebration, I'll give you Rachel. Then for her you'll have to serve me another seven years." Of course, we might think Laban could have found time during seven years to explain the custom. Jacob could rightly ask, "What is this you have done to me? Was it not for Rachel that I served with you? Why then have you deceived me?" (Gen. 29:25) The trickster Jacob had met his match.

Jacob's marital experience was off to a bad start. Two wives, and two maids who would later become Jacob's concubines. Yet God used this strange arrangement for Jacob to father the 12 tribes of Israel. But the picture we're given of domestic tensions in the household make clear it was not God's ideal. Any departure from God's perfect arrangement of one man for one woman (Gen. 2:24) proves enormously difficult. But somehow God works through very imperfect situations to carry out His work in the world.

"So Jacob went in to Rachel also, and indeed he loved Rachel more than Leah, and he served with Laban for another seven years" (Gen. 29:30). We can imagine the anguish of Leah, feeling that she as the older daughter had first right to Jacob. His many little evidences of preference for Rachel would have constantly tortured her.

With most sisters, rivalry ends with marriage. Each daughter marries a man who thinks she is supreme. My two sisters and I have been happily married for many years. One time at a family gathering, my mother pointed out that each husband thought he had acquired the pick of the lot. I noted a look of amazement on the faces of each of the three men. Each expression said as plainly as words, "How could there possibly be any doubt that I got the best one of the three?"

Imagine the anguish of two sisters being married to the same man! The rivalry would last for a lifetime. And Leah's and Rachel's did. No wonder the Mosaic Law later specifically forbade marriage of two sisters to the same man while both were alive. "Neither shalt thou take a wife to her sister . . . to vex her beside the other in her lifetime" (Lev. 18:18, KJV).

"Now the Lord saw that Leah was unloved, and He opened her womb, but Rachel was barren" (Gen. 29:31). In various ways, God compensates in this life. Look hard at the person or family who seems to have everything. Underneath you'll find some secret sorrow, eating away. Or look hard at the person who seems to have little. God gives special joys in suffering. A once-beautiful woman, now hideously crippled up with arthritis, said, "Life is still good. I have my husband, my children, and my home. I still enjoy being alive."

Leah as a Young Mother

So Leah, the unbeautiful, the unloved, was blessed with children. "And Leah conceived and bore a son and named him Reuben, for she said, 'Because the Lord has seen my affliction'" (Gen. 29:32). Leah was learning to look to God rather than to her husband for her heart's needs.

Said Betsey, "The thing that really saved me through those 10 years was that I learned about Christ. Then I knew that Someone really cared about me. I wasn't going through this alone. I joined a Bible study and prayer group that became my support. A Christian neighbor across the street was always there when I needed her. The church was a place where I really belonged, where I found inspiration and strength."

Yet we see Leah as very human in longing for her husband's love. With the birth of her first child, she also said, "'Surely now my husband will love me'" (Gen. 29:32).

Sometimes a woman will trap a man into marriage with a pregnancy. She thinks if she can just get him, she will win his love. Sometimes she does, but it's an uphill battle, requiring the utmost in patience and strength.

"Then she conceived again and bore a son, and said, 'Because the Lord has heard that I am unloved, He has therefore given me this son also.' So she named him Simeon" (Gen. 29:33). The name means "hearing." Leah first thought of her baby in terms of her relationship with God who had heard her prayers.

"And she conceived again and bore a son and said, 'Now this time my husband will become attached to me, because I have borne him three sons.' Therefore he was named Levi" (Gen. 29:34). Levi means "joined." Leah still hoped her husband would give her first place, or at least equal place in his heart. But there's no such thing as equal place for two wives. That's why God has set up marriage to be monogamous (see Gen. 2:24).

"And she conceived again and bore a son and said, 'This time I will praise the Lord.' Therefore she named him Judah. Then she stopped bearing" (Gen. 29:35). Judah means "praise." Had Leah given up on winning her husband's heart? After her fourth son, did she at last turn to God for her joy and sense of acceptance?

Leah as a Sister

When we look at Leah and Rachel as sisters, we don't see a pleasant picture. After Leah had borne four sons and Rachel none, Rachel expressed bitter envy. Leah did not berate Jacob for his lack of love; she turned to God for hope and comfort. But Rachel blamed Jacob for her lack of children. "Now when Rachel saw that she bore Jacob no children, she became jealous of her sister; and she said to Jacob, 'Give me children, or else I die.' Then Jacob's anger burned against Rachel, and he said, 'Am I in the place of God, who has withheld from you the fruit of the womb?'" (Gen. 30:1-2)

Envy, blame, contention, and anger. Not exactly a happy home. Rachel got into the race for children by giving her maid Bilhah to Jacob. According to the laws of Hammurabi, which governed that whole region, this was strictly legal. That didn't make it desirable, or in accordance with God's standards. But legally, Rachel could count her maid's children as her own. So she named the first one Dan, meaning "judging," and said, "God hath judged me"— apparently in the contest with her sister.

Bilhah next produced Naphtali, or "wrestling." The contest was heating up. Rachel saw the baby primarily as a means of catching up with her sister. "With mighty wrestlings I have wrestled with my sister, and I have indeed prevailed" (Gen. 30:8). Not exactly the best emotional climate for babies to come into. No wonder the bitter rivalry between the sisters was carried over to their children. It was the children of Leah who later sold Rachel's child, Joseph, into slavery.

Then Leah became concerned. Since she had lost out on the contest for Jacob's love, she couldn't afford to let Rachel catch up with her in producing children. So she gave her maid Zilpah to Jacob, and Zilpah produced Gad, meaning "a troop." Leah wasn't thinking about God this time; she was only trying to stay ahead in the race. "A troop cometh," she said in choosing a name for Gad. She congratulated herself on finding a way to produce more sons for Jacob. The strategy worked a second time, and Zilpah produced Asher, whose name means "happy." But Leah wasn't thinking of true happiness, the deep-down joy of having been given another son herself by God. She was only thinking of how she would impress other women by acquiring more sons she could call her own. "Happy am I! For women will call me happy" (Gen. 30:13).

We might think Rachel would feel closer to her sister's children than to those of a maid. Envy kept her from enjoying what God had given to someone else. It's not always easy to rejoice with those that rejoice. Envy over the good of another can dissolve all kinds of relationships, as acid eats away at metal.

A trivial incident demonstrates the daily tensions in that household. "Now in the days of wheat harvest Reuben went and found mandrakes in the field, and brought them to his mother Leah. Then Rachel said to Leah, 'Please give me some of your son's mandrakes'" (Gen. 30:14).

The mandrake, a plant growing close to the ground, produces dark green crinkly leaves, and a yellow fruit, shaped like a tomato, about the size of a small plum. The ancients called it a "love apple," and believed it promoted fertility. Little Reuben had brought the fruit to his mother as a child today would bring a bouquet of dandelions. Mandrakes ripened in May or June, "in the days of wheat harvest."

Both Rachel and Leah would have known the popular belief about mandrakes, and both would have wanted the fruit. Leah hadn't borne any children since before her maid Zilpah presented her with two. Rachel hadn't borne any yet. So when Rachel asked for the mandrakes, Leah retorted, "Is it a small matter for you to take my husband? And would you take my son's mandrakes also?" (Gen. 30:15)

We all make efforts at self-control. Yet we all know we can't live close to others without sooner or later blurting out our true feelings. If we don't want bitterness to pop out, we'd better get our feelings straightened out. Ultimately, feelings can't be covered up.

Rachel bargained with Leah for Jacob's attentions. "Therefore he may lie with you tonight in return for your son's mandrakes" (Gen. 30:15). So Rachel traded one night with her husband for something believed to possess magic qualities. We get the picture. Leah lived in her tent surrounded by her children. Zilpah and Bilhah each had a tent. And Rachel lived in her own tent with Jacob (Gen. 31:33). But for one night Leah was to have him. "When Jacob came in from the field in the evening, then Leah went out to meet him and said, 'You must come in to me, for I have surely hired you with my son's mandrakes.' So he lay with her that night. And God gave heed to Leah, and she conceived and bore Jacob a fifth son" (Gen. 30:16-17).

Notice, it was the wife who gave up the mandrakes who became pregnant. The popular faith in mandrakes did nothing for Rachel.

It appears that Leah's spirituality sagged a little in the race for children. "Then Leah said, 'God has given me my wages, because I gave my maid to my husband.' So she named him Issachar" (Gen. 30:18), which means "hire." She already had four sons, plus two by her maid. Now God gave her a fifth of her own. She congratulated herself, and imagined God was rewarding her for giving up her own pleasure to let her maid conceive a son by Jacob.

"And Leah conceived again and bore a sixth son to Jacob. Then Leah said, 'God has endowed me with a good gift; now my husband will dwell with me, because I have borne him six sons," (Gen. 30:19-20).

Poor Leah never gave up hope that her childbearing prowess would earn her husband's love. She still hoped he would spend his time in her tent, not in Rachel's. "So she named him Zebulun," which means "dwelling" (Gen. 30:20).

Many a couple have been disappointed in the hope that a baby would bring them closer together. Says a popular psychologist, "A child will make a good marriage better, and a bad marriage worse." We can imagine how Leah's children resented Jacob's habitual absence from their tent. Their sense of neglect showed in their violent behavior later on. Joseph, who showed such wonderful qualities, enjoyed the presence, love, and esteem of his father.

Many a wife without any children has been tenderly loved by her husband. Jacob was right. It is God who gives or withholds the blessing and burden of children (Gen. 30:2). Rachel was loved before she had children. She was also loved afterward.

Leah as Daughter

Leah never captured her husband's fancy in the way that Rachel did. But she came to a place of some equality and acceptance. When Jacob was planning to leave Laban to go back to his own land, he "sent and called Rachel and Leah to his flock in the field" (Gen. 31:4). No doubt he didn't want the conversation overheard. He consulted with both, concerned himself with the feelings and opinions of both.

For once Leah and Rachel were united. Both felt their father had cheated their husband.

"And Rachel and Leah answered and said to him, 'Do we still have any portion or inheritance in our father's house? Are we not reckoned by him as foreigners? For he has sold us, and has also entirely consumed our purchase price. Surely all the wealth which God has taken away from our father belongs to us and our children; now then, do whatever God has said to you'" (Gen. 31:14-16).

So both, in a conflict between father and husband, sided with the husband—as loyal wives. They agreed to leave their father's household to go back to Canaan with Jacob. "So he fled with all that he had" (Gen. 31:21).

Laban pursued and overtook Jacob. They settled their differences, agreed not to hurt each other in the future, and then gathered stones into a heap as a sign of their covenant. The mound was called *Mizpah,* or "watchtower," for Laban said, "May the Lord watch between you and me when we are absent one from the other. . . . This heap is a witness . . . that I will not pass by this heap to you for harm, and you will not pass by this heap and this pillar to me, for harm. The God of Abraham . . . and of Nahor . . . judge between us" (Gen. 31:49-53).

Not a bad idea to set a symbolic heap of stones between in-laws, in promise that neither will invade the other's territory. One very sensitive and conscientious daughter-in-law went to see her pastor about how to handle her mother-in-law. The mother loved her son's wife so much that she wanted to be with her all the time. She wanted to share every task, sit with her when she sat, go out socially when she went out, shop with her when she shopped. The daughter-in-law felt suffocated.

The pastor suggested that they draw a boundary line between them. The daughter-in-law was to state frankly her need for some privacy. The mother was to develop some interests and an independent life of her own. They lived happily together for many years with their "watchtower" between them. Sometimes in-laws who can't stand total togetherness get along fine if each allows the other his own territory.

Laban went back to Paddan-aram. As Jacob and his entourage drew close to Canaan, Leah endured one more jab to her feelings. She lived with constant reminders that Jacob loved Rachel more.

Esau was approaching with a band of 400 men. Jacob feared an attack on his household. He went on before, but in the procession he put the handmaids and their children first, then Leah and her children, then Rachel and Joseph "last" (Gen. 33:2)—in the most protected position.

Leah as an Older Mother

Once they arrived in the land of Canaan, Leah's griefs with her children began. Her daughter Dinah "went out to visit the daughters of the land" (Gen. 34:1), in the nearby pagan city. Of course Jacob should have used better judgment than to camp so near to such a place. The prince of the country saw Dinah and violated her. Afterward he wanted to marry her. But her brothers, feeling insulted by such treatment of their sister, deceived and then murdered all the men of the city. After the disaster Jacob seemed more troubled by the ensuing threat to his own safety than by what had happened to his daughter, or by what his sons had done. "Then Jacob said to Simeon and Levi, 'You have brought trouble on me, by making me odious among the inhabitants of the land, among the Canaanites and the Perizzites; and my men being few in number, they will gather together against me and attack me and I shall be destroyed, I and my household.' But they said, 'Should he treat our sister as a harlot?'" (Gen. 34:30-31)

Do we glimpse here the lack of a father's firm hand among Leah's children? Certainly the brothers sensed Jacob's lack of concern for Dinah. They, rather than he, felt responsible for her honor. How much better if Jacob had brought mature judgment to the solution of this bad situation!

Said Betsey, "The most painful thing to me is Allan's lack of interest in the children. The children's hurt is worse than my own. My daughter says, 'Daddy left us.' He doesn't do the seeking. He thinks that they should seek him. They have to do the calling. My son won a big contest in Bible memorization. He'd been working toward it for months, but his father didn't take the trouble to be there, or even to call and inquire how it went. My son, a big guy, 18 years old, said, 'Dad's a great guy. I wish I could see him sometime.' And then he sat there crying.

Said Wilma, "The children—his two and my two—have gone through some rough times as a result of our divorces. I had a lot of trouble with my role as stepmother. When my husband's daughter came to live with us at age nine, for about a year she constantly challenged my authority. Because of my own insecurities from past failures, I had terrible doubts of my self-worth and was very defensive. I've now learned how to deal with failure. After about a year, she became my right arm. Evelyn and I did everything together. She was like a little mother; she enjoyed running the household while I was at work. At 12, she could cook whole meals—meat loaf, pork chops, vegetables, salad, dessert, she could make it all come together. I would reward her with special little things.

"My older son Philip was devastated after the divorce. Before I married again, he became the father of the family, assuming all the protective type of duties. Bill, my former husband, had taken Philip with him through his escapades with women, even into the bedroom. He was proud of his dad's macho image and thought he could get by with anything. Philip blamed me for the divorce, feeling I should just go along and accept things as they were.

"Philip was agreeable when I married again. But two years later when my husband's two children came to live with us, he felt overwhelmed and said, 'Mom, you don't need me anymore.' He went to live with his father. When he returned to me as a senior in high school, he had become a different person—rebellious, dirty, with long hair and beard, unable to hold a job. He was so rebellious that everyone thought he would never get it together. I hate to say it but I was ashamed of Philip. For me it was another failure.

"Now he has worked through his anger, and is established in business for himself. He can't do enough for me. Recently, he told me about all those experiences his father subjected him to, and apologized for what he had put me through. He frequently invites me out to lunch. I say, give a young person time—be always the same, always available, and he'll eventually come back. Don't give up. Allow a child to go through this unexplainable portion of his life. If he can believe that your actions will match your words, he'll come through. When everything was falling apart for Philip, no job and no money to make car payments, I helped him financially.

"He was like the prodigal son in going away, then coming back. I tried always to show him that I believed in him. It's so easy for parents to be negative all the time, forgetting about the positive. You have to show them the way, not criticize.

"My younger son didn't seem to suffer from the divorce. Children differ in the way they take things. He was always happy, always loving—like a teddy bear.

"Jim's younger son has gone through a heavy drug problem. But he's on his way out now.

"A split family is a very special family. All of the children need a great deal of love and understanding. Sometimes you just have to stand back and wait for them to get their feelings straightened out. They go through some very difficult times.

"A split family is pulled in so many different directions. After carrying responsibility for four children all year, Jim and I awakened Christmas morning to a quiet house—the children were with their other parents.

"But when I manage to have all my children lined up with me in church, I think, 'I won! They've all come through their terrible struggles.' And when they're all together at a family gathering—a birthday, Mother's Day—it's paradise for me.

"When my younger son graduated from college, everybody was there—my folks, Bill's folks, Bill and his present wife and three children, my husband Jim and our four children, and all their boyfriends and girlfriends. All got along beautifully.

"I treat Jim's first wife pleasantly, politely, even though she has a very threatening effect on me. But she's a definite part of her children's lives. She *is* their mother. Evelyn used to say, 'Mom was over again today. I wish she wouldn't bother me so much.' But I never ask her not to come.

"The two Bible study groups that Jim and I attend are a great support to us. I'd go to more if I had time. My strong family background gave me the strength to go through all this. My parents read the Bible, prayed, and disciplined us firmly. If I was too sick to go to church, I was too sick to go anywhere else at all that day. My father talked to us a lot about life, living by the golden rule, sharing, and getting along with people. He was very outspoken about right and wrong. I really thank them and thank the Lord for making it possible for me to survive all this. It hasn't been easy.

"There are a lot of difficult times in a complex relationship—but if you keep your eye on the ultimate goal, you're going to make it. You have to keep your mind on the other person's needs. You learn to appreciate, to emphasize the positive. You learn how to feel good about yourself. It's so easy to fall into the failure syndrome—'I'm not going to succeed anyway, so why try?'

"My own inward hurt made me reach out to others. I learned that if you smile hard enough, you can keep the tears back. When you have been deeply hurt yourself, you can feel with others."

Leah too won out in the end. After Rachel died, Leah probably enjoyed a closer relationship with Jacob. One feels a certain tenderness in Jacob's words at the end of his life: "There I buried Leah" (Gen. 49:31). To this day you can visit the place in Hebron where tradition says Leah's body lies beside Jacob's. Rachel was buried elsewhere, but Leah occupied the ancestral burial ground. There lie also Abraham and Sarah, and Isaac and Rebekah.

Leah didn't live to see it, but in the end Reuben and her other sons were beautifully reconciled to Rachel's son Joseph. When they met Joseph again, as vice-regent of Egypt, he said to his half-brothers, "Now do not be grieved nor angry with yourselves, because you sold me here; for God sent me before you to preserve life. . . . It was not you who sent me here, but God" (Gen. 45:5-8).

A split family is not an ideal family, of course. Yet God can overrule all mistakes, and bring blessing out of evil and suffering. Leah became the ancestress of Christ, through her son Judah, who himself made plenty of mistakes, and yet was chosen to be in the line of the Messiah.

8
How to Survive
as a Single Parent

"So a truck has run over you. You can either lie down and die, or get up and live. Which are you going to do, Carol?" Gladys Griffy asked this question in the worst moment of her friend Carol's life. That worst moment was when Carol saw her marriage disintegrating, after three children and 14 years of marriage.

In the past 10 years the proportion of U.S. households consisting of a single parent with children has increased from five to over seven percent of the total number of households.

How does the single mother cope? Like the widow of Zarephath, she faces certain problems. She works these out according to various procedures, and in her mind entertains certain prospects. Along the way she must make choices. We'll look at four aspects of the single parent's life—problems, procedures and prospects, choices, and faith.

Problems

Barbara, another divorcée and single parent, depends upon the Lord for strength "to keep always on the move." Says Barbara, "When I drive home from work, I feel so tired. I just ask the Lord for strength to see me through cooking the supper, meeting my children's needs, washing dishes, cleaning, and shopping. The hardest part is having to be always doing something."

Many a single mother today barely gets along. She makes do on what she earns, plus what a husband has left in insurance, or what one who has walked off may pay in child support. The precarious financial balance is constantly threatened by inflation, some big expense, an illness, or a temporary loss of work. Like the widow of Zarephath, a single parent knows present and impending problems—the problem of bringing up a child or children alone. She knows the burden of being responsible for every little thing herself—paying the gas bill, figuring the income tax, getting washers for the faucets, reading a story to a child, taking him on an outing, praying and talking to each child, and tucking each in for the night. She faces the constant need for courage to go on with the struggle of life.

Gertrude's husband died of cancer at age 36. "He had a wonderful position as head car designer, and worked up until five weeks before he died. I kept him at home until one week before his death.

"The best thing for me was that no one babied me. My minister visited me on Saturday, the day after the funeral. He told me to come to church the next day—it wouldn't be any easier a month later. My doctor refused to give me any drugs, though I didn't sleep for a week. He said when I was tired enough I would sleep. Step by step the Lord led me along. I brought up three wonderful daughters. I came out better than some families with two parents."

God has always looked out for the widow. He provided special care for one widow when He directed Elijah to stay in her home. He said to Elijah, "Arise, go to Zarephath, which belongs to Sidon, and stay there; behold, I have commanded a widow there to provide for you" (1 Kings 17:9).

Elijah had appeared before the wicked King Ahab like a flash of lightning, coming from nowhere, seemingly disappearing to nowhere. "As the Lord, the God of Israel lives, before whom I stand, surely there shall be neither dew nor rain these years, except by my word" (1 Kings 17:1). Jezebel, Ahab's wife, was zealously trying to convert Israel to Baalism. People worshiped Baal as god of nature and fertility, the one who was in control of the rain. Elijah publicly defied Baal when he claimed that the Lord God of Israel controlled the rain. And we learn from James 5:17 that

Elijah had actually prayed that it might not rain, and it didn't rain for three and one-half years. Evidently, Elijah felt that drought was what people needed to bring them back to God.

Imagine the pressure on Elijah as the country sank deeper and deeper into drought and starvation. How could he have stood the importunities of the people, the threats of the king? The Lord told him it was a time to keep silent. "Go away from here and turn eastward, and hide yourself by the Brook Cherith, which is east of the Jordan" (1 Kings 17:3).

There, through miraculous provision and in solitude, God prepared Elijah for his great test on Mount Carmel. At times, we all need to grow in the Lord by being shut away from the life of action. One time I was at home for months on end with illness. I couldn't do anything for the Lord's work except pray and encourage my pastor husband. At the time, I assumed the church would really suffer because I couldn't teach my Bible classes. It didn't. Good substitutes were found, the church roared along marvelously without me. There were some lessons from solitude I needed to learn. Those months proved a time of tremendous spiritual growth. I already possessed head knowledge of Scripture; what I learned was heart knowledge. God met my needs, and those of my husband and four little children from day to day, during very difficult circumstances.

No doubt Elijah didn't much favor moving from the court of a king to a hiding place in the wilderness. He must have felt some trauma at leaving the center of drama and conflict. In the wilderness he had nothing much to do except wait for some ravens to bring his next meal. When he needed it, he dipped a little water from the stream nearby. He lived in the limestone caves of the ravine, moved about among the dense foliage growing along the watercourse deep in the ravine.

He watched the water in that stream gradually diminish. Finally, the drought dried it up. God wrought no miracle to supply the prophet with water. Elijah wasn't told what to do next until after the stream ran dry.

Each single parent has seen one source of provision—a partner who shared responsibility—dry up. Each must look for some other source. Elijah waited for the Word of God before leaving the dried-up streambed. Then he moved on to the next stage in his life.

"Arise, go to Zarephath, which belongs to Sidon, and stay there; behold, I have commanded a widow there to provide for you" (1 Kings 17:9).

Dreary as the ravine in the wilderness was, Elijah would have questioned God's next move. How could God possibly want him to go to Zarephath—right in Jezebel's own home territory? Her father Ethbaal still reigned as king there. Zarephath lay on the shore of the Mediterranean, on the road between Tyre and Sidon, only seven miles from Sidon itself.

Furthermore, Elijah certainly must have questioned why God would suggest that a *widow* there would feed him. Widows in that society stood notoriously in need themselves. Throughout Scripture, God showed special concern for the overwhelming needs of widows. The widow was to be included, along with the stranger, in the general provision (Deut. 14:29; 16:11, 14). She was not to be taken advantage of. Any grain or olives or grapes left after the first gathering were to be left for the stranger, for the fatherless, and for the widow. (See Deut. 24:19-21.) Job cited as one of his virtues that he "made the widow's heart sing for joy" (Job 29:13). The psalmist rejoiced in God's care for the widow (Ps. 146:9). In the early church, one of the first concerns was care for widows (Acts 6:1).

Many a widow has claimed for herself God's words to Israel, "For your husband is your Maker, whose name is the Lord of hosts; and your Redeemer is the Holy One of Israel, who is called the God of all the earth" (Isa. 54:5). One widow said, "When I came upon that verse, it spoke to me. I realized that God had been like a husband to me, providing, directing, loving me. I know I have nothing to fear because of His concern for me."

How could Elijah expect a widow to feed him? Yet "he arose and went to Zarephath" (1 Kings 17:10). To go straight to Zarephath on the Mediterranean shore, Elijah would have to pass the summer palace of Ahab and Jezebel at Jezreel, and come very close to the capital city of Samaria. To avoid these places of danger, he probably traveled north along the Jordan past the Sea of Galilee. He might then have cut across the southern portion of Phenicia to reach the coast. A trip of about 100 miles—five full days of walking.

On the way to Zarephath, Elijah passed the homes of many worthy widows. Jesus said so, that day He preached in the synagogue at Nazareth. "There were many widows in Israel in the days of Elijah, when the sky was shut up for three years and six months, when a great famine came over all the land; and yet Elijah was sent to none of them, but only to Zarephath in the land of Sidon, to a woman who was a widow" (Luke 4:25-26).

Why was Elijah directed to ask an impossible thing of a poor widow in a heathen land? God intended to open up a new life to this Gentile woman, as well as to teach Elijah more lessons. He wished to show Elijah that even among the hated Baal worshipers, there lived hungry souls—people who suffered, who longed to be loved—people potentially open to God. He wants us to learn not to put people into categories, but to look at them as individuals. He wanted to teach the widow that giving can open the way to a new life.

Elijah had watched the water in the brook fail. The widow had seen some brooks fail in her life too. Her husband had died. Probably, she was just eking out a living for herself and her son, when the famine in Israel at last touched Phenicia (Lebanon). The Greek historian Menander mentioned a famine of a year's duration at that time in ancient Phenicia.

Water in that part of the world is a precious commodity. Israelis are now piping water out of the Sea of Galilee to bring the southern Negev to life. But they have to negotiate carefully with the country of Jordan as to how much they're allowed to take. Israelis cover over every spring of water, for too much will evaporate if the water is allowed to flow uncovered. Each year they can count on three months of rain in the winter—the early rains. In good years they enjoy "latter rains" in the spring. But in the time of Elijah, they went three and one-half years without any rain at all, not even the heavy dews with which they could produce some crops.

You can still find ruins of ancient Zarephath or Sarepta. The city lives on as a miserable little village called Surafend. This name means "furnaces or workshops" for the refining of metals. Both Elijah and the widow went through some refining experiences there.

"And when he came to the gate of the city, behold, a widow was there gathering sticks" (1 Kings 17:10). She had to be poor to be scrounging about outside the city gate for a few twigs. Her dress would mark her as a widow; it would also mark her as poor.

"And he called to her and said, 'Please get me a little water in a jar, that I may drink'" (1 Kings 17:10). Likewise, Abraham's servant, in search of a bride for Isaac, asked for a drink of water (Gen. 24:17). So did Jesus in search of turning a woman's heart to Himself (John 4:7). It was a sacred duty in that region to give even the last drop of water in the desert to a stranger. But it certainly was a test for Elijah to have to ask food of a heathen widow who was destitute.

"And as she was going to get it, he called to her and said, 'Please bring me a piece of bread in your hand.' But she said, 'As the Lord your God lives, I have no bread, only a handful of flour in the bowl and a little oil in the jar; and behold, I am gathering a few sticks that I may go in and prepare for me and my son, that we may eat it and die'" (1 Kings 17:11-12).

Procedures and Prospects

In the face of special problems, each single mother develops certain procedures. And each has in mind certain prospects for herself and her children.

Said Gertrude, whose husband died, "My one objective was to keep the home as much as possible as it had been. I had some insurance, some social security, and I settled for a job in a school lunchroom because it took me away from home only four hours a day. The job didn't pay much, but I was home vacations and afternoons when my children were home. I had to do everything myself—painting, paperhanging, sewing, repairing—to make ends meet. I had to always be so busy for so many years, that now I can't sit still. When the third daughter went to college, I took a full-time job as an office manager. I fill up my evenings with church activities. I think keeping busy keeps the devil away. I believe in work as therapy. I didn't have time to feel sorry for myself."

Said Carol, "When I saw my marriage breaking up, my husband staying out whole nights, ignoring me and the children, I would lie on the couch for whole days and cry. I had read books about marriage, tried in every way I knew to keep my marriage alive. I begged my husband, for the sake of our 14 years together, and for the children, to go for counseling. Everything seemed of no avail. I was tired, run-down, and lost a lot of weight. I asked a pastor how long I should hang in there. He said, 'Until it begins to destroy you.'

"Finally, I said to my husband, 'It looks like our marriage is over.'

"He said, 'It's been over for a long time.'

"We had recently moved to a strange city for a job for my husband. I had no friends or relatives there, nothing except my church. I remembered my daughter's Sunday School teacher had said to me, 'If you ever need anyone to talk to, call me.'

"So I called Gladys. That was when she said to me, 'You can either lie down and die, or get up and live.' I decided to get up and live."

The widow of Zarephath had considered all possible procedures, and decided to lie down and die. Her prospects appeared nil until Elijah came. And he had the nerve to ask her to share the one batch of meal and oil she had left—not only to share, but to give to him first.

The widow of Zarephath must have shrunk from giving of her last morsel. But Elijah commanded it. "Do not fear; go, do as you have said, but make me a little bread cake from it first, and bring it out to me, and afterward you may make one for yourself and for your son. For thus says the Lord God of Israel, 'The bowl of flour shall not be exhausted, nor shall the jar of oil be empty, until the day that the Lord sends rain on the face of the earth'" (1 Kings 17:13-14).

God asks us to give for our own good. He looks not at the size of the gift, but at its quality. Jesus ignored the rich people casting in of their abundance, and pointed out a poor widow who put in her two mites, all she had (Luke 21:1-4). God looks at our gift in terms of what we have left after we've given. Giving unleashes God's capacity to give to us.

Says Carol, "Our budget doesn't balance on paper. I don't earn enough; I'm not given enough in child support to make ends meet. But I take the tithe off first, and miraculously, I always have enough to pay the bills. I sold my diamond, and got way more than I expected. That paid the lawyer's fees. On the bulletin board at church I found the name of a girl who wanted to rent a room. That helps with taxes and house payments. And she's good company. And sometimes money just comes through the mail from somebody who thinks I might need it."

Barbara, who is German by birth, described the same experience of God's provision. "Right after my divorce, I didn't have enough to get along on, but in miraculous little ways, the Lord provided. For example, the first summer a lot of people in my condominium ordered macrame plant-hangers which I made. I had just enough income to pay my rent and buy food. Money from those plant-hangers took care of car repairs, clothing, and extras. Then I began baby-sitting and that developed into running a licensed child care center. When my children got to school age, the nursery work seemed more than I could handle emotionally. At that time, a full-time job at the church was offered to me. I love everybody there so much, and feel so loved. It was a miracle how the job came to me. After I joined the church, I volunteered to help in the office one Saturday a month. That was while I was running the child care center five days a week. I had been a secretary in Germany, but never in this country. With only a little experience in office work here, I suppose office managers feared I couldn't handle the work in English. But at the church they gave me time to make the transition."

Choices

Barbara, Carol, Gertrude—and the widow of Zarephath—all faced problems. All saw possibilities. Each had to make a choice. The widow of Zarephath could have turned her back on Elijah.

Barbara could have said she didn't want to do volunteer work, that she needed to be paid.

Carol could have said she had to go back to her hometown, that she couldn't stay in a strange city. "I might have gone back into my old cocoon of family, friends, and an apathetic church. I did find a job when I visited there. But when I came back to Livonia to sell my house and pack, I sat in church and cried at the thought of leaving. I found I couldn't bear to leave the church where I had found a big new family in Christ. There's so much support here.

"Praying that God would open the way for me to stay, I told the head of our singles group at the church that I needed a job. Five minutes later a man came up to him and said he was looking for an administrative assistant. I applied and was hired on the basis of my experience in volunteer work—I had directed 90 volunteers. I got another job offer that same day, and had an interview for the next day. So I knew God wanted me to stay. But it was a great big step of faith."

The widow of Zarephath searched the face of that wild-looking prophet and made her choice. No doubt Elijah had the long hair of a Nazarite, and was dressed like a Bedouin from the desert, with a garment of coarse camel's hair, and a leather girdle (2 Kings 1:8). He also wore the mantle of his prophetic office (2 Kings 2:8, 13). And he spoke with authority. "For thus says the Lord God of Israel, 'The bowl of flour shall not be exhausted nor shall the jar of oil be empty, until the day that the Lord sends rain on the face of the earth'" (1 Kings 17:14).

Faith

The widow of Zarephath took the chance—"she went and did according to the word of Elijah" (1 Kings 17:15). She stepped out on faith. Said Carol, "I've found that when you walk through one door, the Lord opens the next door before you. You have to take that step of faith."

There are spiritual laws that operate opposite from the way most people think life works. "Give, and it will be given to you. . . . For whatever measure you deal out to others, it will be dealt to you in return" (Luke 6:38). "There is one who scatters, yet increases" (Prov. 11:24).

The widow gave Elijah a little cake of meal that was so costly at that time. As a result, she and her child were provided for during the rest of the famine. Elijah stayed in the upper room of her little stone house, in a room built on the flat roof with an outside stairway leading to it. "And she and he and her household ate for many days. The bowl of flour was not exhausted nor did the jar of oil become empty, according to the Word of the Lord which He spoke through Elijah" (1 Kings 17:15-16).

The Lord provided steadily, daily, in little undramatic ways—as many of us have seen Him provide. But again tragedy struck. Most of us have discovered that life never goes along on an even keel for any great length of time. Apparently, we need storms and stresses to grow on. "Now it came about after these things, that the son of the woman, the mistress of the house, became sick; and his sickness was so severe, that there was no breath left in him" (1 Kings 17:17).

Out the window flew all thoughts of God's provision so far. By now, having food to eat seemed routine. Anyway, what does food to keep yourself alive matter if your only son lies dead? To this widow, her son represented not only present joy, but future prospects. She counted on him to provide for her old age, to fill her life with the warmth and pleasure of grandchildren. Through him alone could she feel a part of ongoing life. Now he lay lifeless.

Single parents face special kinds of dying in regard to their children. Sons and daughters may take out their grief for a dead or departed parent on the one who remains. One mother said, "My 13-year-old daughter is in full rebellion against me and my other children. She is threatening to go and live with her father who is moving a thousand miles away. He didn't pay much attention to her when he was married to me. And his lifestyle isn't a good example to her. But I have to accept this if this is what she wants to do, and trust God that good can come out of it." God can bring resurrection out of all kinds of deaths.

The widow of Zarephath responded to her loss with a very human outburst. "What do I have to do with you, O man of God?

You have come to me to bring my iniquity to remembrance, and to put my son to death!" (1 Kings 17:18) The widow forgot all about Elijah's kindness in coming to reside with her. Ancient peoples commonly regarded the presence of a prophet in the home as a source of blessing. Instead, this widow felt the prophet's presence had called God's attention to her sin, and that she was being punished. She blamed Elijah for her son's death, forgetting that she had expected that both she and her son would die from lack of food long before this.

What sin in her life do you suppose the widow was thinking of? Perhaps just a general feeling of guilt. Perhaps she thought of things she should have done, or things she should not have done in regard to her husband. Part of every grief is regret and guilt. Perhaps she condemned herself for rebelling in her heart against God because she was a widow. Psychiatrists say most of their practice deals with the problem of guilt. Humanly speaking, they can do nothing about it—except to help patients bring it out into the open and look at it. Only Christ can take care of our sense of guilt. He can rid us of true guilt for things we have really done that were wrong. He can also free us from false guilt based on a general feeling of unworthiness.

Imagine Elijah's feelings. In the wilderness ravine, over there by the Jordan, Elijah had learned the lessons of solitude, living with God face to face. In this house in Zarephath, he was learning the lessons of fellowship—of becoming involved with individuals, of caring. He not only had to learn the lesson that God could provide for him, he also had to share in the suffering brought on by the drought, and see how it affected people.

Elijah suffered with the widow to whom he had promised sustenance throughout the drought. He suffered personal grief for the child. Elijah didn't argue with the woman about whether she should blame him for the child's death. He was too involved himself. " 'Give me your son.' Then he took him from her bosom and carried him up to the upper room where he was living, and laid him on his own bed. And he called to the Lord and said, 'O Lord my God, hast Thou also brought calamity to the widow with whom I am staying, by causing her son to die?' " (1 Kings 17:19-20)

Elijah didn't rebuke the woman for her complaints; he had some complaints against God himself. But he didn't voice them to the woman—he took them directly to God. And he threw his whole soul into bringing the boy back to life. "He stretched himself upon the child three times, and called to the Lord, and said, 'O Lord my God, I pray Thee, let this child's life return to him'" (1 Kings 17:21).

We have many instances today of people who have apparently been dead for a matter of minutes and then have been revived. My own sister was rushed to a hospital one night with a heart attack. Her heart had stopped. They thumped her chest, put her on machines, and injected drugs. After a few hours, two of the three doctors wanted to give up. The third said, "Let's keep on a little longer." They worked over her from early evening till dawn. Her minister, her husband, and others were in the hall praying. Today she's alive and well, and caring for her family. She is active in volunteer work, travels, swims, and enjoys life.

Elijah didn't just request that God heal the child. He involved himself in the project as God's means to do it. He spared no effort, but stretched himself upon the child once, twice, and three times. This number of the Trinity suggests God in all His fullness and power.

This story is not only an historical happening. Like other miracles of Scripture, it is also a parable. Each of us has the privilege from time to time of being an Elijah—God's means of bringing a dead soul to life in Christ. "And you hath He quickened who were dead in your trespasses and sins" (Eph. 2:1, NIV). Said one such who was brought to life, "That's really true. I was really dead before I found Christ."

We, like Elijah, bring people to life by becoming thoroughly involved. Involved in God's Word, so that it becomes a power in us, working through us. Involved in people, so that they can feel and experience the love of God through us.

"And the Lord heard the voice of Elijah, and the life of the child returned to him and he revived" (1 Kings 17:22).

One time a man slumped down in church during the closing hymn. A woman in the choir saw him fall and dashed out for a doctor whom she knew to be teaching a young married couples' class. The doctor went straight to the man, found his heart had stopped, and began thumping his chest. The heart started up again. "You really have to pound to get a heart started again. It's possible to even break a rib in the effort," the doctor later said.

They rushed the man to the hospital of course. The next Sunday he was in church again. God worked a miracle in that boy of Zarephath. He still works miracles in people's lives, sometimes physically, often spiritually.

"And Elijah took the child, and brought him down from the upper room into the house and gave him to his mother; and Elijah said, 'See, your son is alive'" (1 Kings 17:23).

Imagine Elijah's joy. And imagine the mother's immediate joy in the child, and future hope for her life. "Then the woman said to Elijah, 'Now I know that you are a man of God, and that the Word of the Lord in your mouth is truth'" (1 Kings 17:24).

Notice the widow's growth in faith. She had a kind of faith in Jehovah before the prophet came. "As the Lord your God lives . . ." (1 Kings 17:12). Perhaps she believed in both Jehovah and Baal. The people of Tyre knew nothing of monotheism.

At first she had accepted the prophet as one who might provide food for her. But her faith didn't grow very much through having the prophet in her home. The first thing that went wrong, she blamed him and God, and took no account of her blessings up to that time.

But when she saw God bring life out of death, she accepted Elijah's message about God as the truth. The greatest miracle in the world is a changed life. You and I have seen it over and over again. Each time it is a fresh proof of the truth and power of God's Word.

Said Carol, "I asked God, 'Why did you take everything away from me? You took my home. I lived in a 50-year-old house that I loved. You took my friends, at the same time you took my pride. When my husband's business failed and he went through bankruptcy, people I'd known all my life snubbed me. You took my family and relatives. I had to move away from my childhood home because of my husband's work. You took my community volunteer work, which I loved so much. You took the church of my childhood, with all its associations. Why did You bring me out here to Detroit? There I even lost my husband. Then I lost my health—even my curly hair. The texture changed. I even lost all our Christmas decorations which the kids and I had made through the years. They were important to us. They got water-soaked in the basement. Why did You do all this to me?'

"I know the answer. I'm a very stubborn person. He allowed it all to happen so that I would learn to look only to Him. I might never have come to know Him otherwise. I really praise God for all that has happened to me. He loves me enough to want me.

"I was an achiever, always wanting to make an impression. Others came to me for strength. My strength finally ran out. Now I'm tapped into a source of love and strength that will never run out. My maiden name was Good. But now I'm much better. And someday I'll be the best. I'm through with the struggle of trying to get to heaven on my good works. I revel in the miracle that God loves me for myself."

In just such a way, the widow of Zarephath saw God work in her life. God drew her to Himself so that she, like Carol, Barbara, and Gertrude, could witness firsthand God's power to restore life.

9
How Not to Be
an Influence for Bad

Tim happily told us he had found the girl he wanted to marry. Tim ushered regularly at church and worked conscientiously in several other jobs around the church. His fiancée was very attached to her own religion. But she would attend church with him, he assured us, after they were married.

The wedding came and went. Tim continued to worship with us for a few months, then gradually disappeared. His fiancée came once with him to talk with his pastor, but she never attended a worship service. We haven't seen him now for several years.

From time immemorial, wives have been influencing their husbands, for better or for worse. Jezebel wielded enormous power for evil. She corrupted a whole nation through her influence on her husband. Few wives have access to so large a sphere But all share the opportunity to affect their husbands, their children, their church, or community. How did Jezebel wield her power so effectively? What can we learn from her, both positively and negatively?

We see in Jezebel and Ahab the tragic results of being unequally yoked together with an unbeliever (2 Cor. 6:14). We see the relative dominance of personalities, regardless of whether male or female. We see the awful consequences of commitment to evil versus the wonderful consequences of commitment to God. We see the power of single-minded dedication to an objective. Unfortunately, most of us dissipate our energies by moving in several directions at once.

We'll look at Jezebel's identity, her objective, her methods, and her results.

Jezebel's Identity

Who was Jezebel? We meet her as the wife of King Ahab. "Ahab the son of Omri became king over Israel in the 38th year of Asa king of Judah. . . . And it came about, as though it had been a trivial thing for him to walk in the sins of Jeroboam the son of Nebat, that he married Jezebel the daughter of Ethbaal king of the Sidonians" (1 Kings 16:29, 31).

Jezebel's name has become a byword for evil. The dictionary defines it capitalized as "the wife of Ahab," and uncapitalized as "a shameless and daring woman." By the time John wrote the Book of Revelation, 1,000 years after Jezebel, her name had become a byword for apostasy. In Revelation it designates a woman who seduced others into fornication and idolatry.

Part of Jezebel's power over Ahab and others was her strong sense of identity. She knew who she was. She was daughter of Ethbaal, king of the Zidonians or Phoenicians, which is the area of modern Lebanon. Ethbaal gained the throne by killing his brother, who in turn had killed the last king of Hiram's dynasty. Ethbaal's name means "Baal is with him," or "Man of Baal." Fanatically devoted to Baal, he named his daughter Jezebel, for his god.

Ahab, king of Israel, knew better than to marry a Canaanite. God had warned that such an alliance could become a scourge. It was totally contrary to the Law of God. When Ethbaal gave his daughter to the equal or less powerful king of Israel, he no doubt wrote some requirements into the contract. For he would have wanted Baal to be worshiped in Israel.

The marriage was an act of policy on both sides. Israel wanted to secure itself against Syria and Assyria. Sidon was a great trade center, with ships and overland caravans coming and going. It was wealthy, immoral, cultured, cosmopolitan. It must have appealed to the pride of Israel's king and people alike to secure as their queen such a princess as Jezebel. She would bring prestige and pomp, wealth and luxury, to the simpler and more staid life of Israel.

But she also brought Baalism. Baal, a chief male deity of the Canaanite pantheon, was the god of agriculture. He it was who gave increase to family and field, flocks and herds. Baal worship was conducted with pompous rituals in temples, by priests in splendid vestments. Today you can visit the magnificent ruins of one of these temples at Baalbek, Lebanon. It's unbelievably huge and impressive.

In good weather, Baal was also worshiped outdoors, especially on "high places"—hilltops. He was worshiped with animal sacrifices, ritualistic meals, and above all with licentious rites. Since he was the god of fertility, worshipers engaged in sacred prostitution, with both male and female temple prostitutes. The profits went to the temple.

Archeologists have found many remains of Baalism that help us to understand why God told Israel to have nothing to do with the religion of the Canaanites. (See Deut. 7:1-6.)

At Megiddo, not far from Samaria, in a layer of earth from Ahab's time, they found a temple of Asherah, goddess wife of Baal. Nearby they uncovered a cemetery with many jars containing the remains of infants that had evidently been sacrificed in the temple.

Jezebel brought with her from Tyre and Sidon a retinue of "450 prophets of Baal and 400 prophets of the Asherah" (1 Kings 18:19). Imagine the temple and the apartments Ahab had to build to accommodate all of these. They "ate at Jezebel's table," were luxuriously housed and dined at Israelite taxpayers' expense. The prestige these prophets enjoyed living so close to the queen affected everyone in the nation.

We can learn from Jezebel the importance of a strong sense of identity. Each one of us is a child of God, created in the image of God, potentially redeemable by Christ, and put in this world to accomplish something for Him. As we grow closer to Him, and learn better who we are, we gain a desirable sense of identity.

Jezebel's Objective

Secure in her identity, Jezebel stood just as firmly in her objective. She sought to convert Israel to Baalism.

Israelite kings had already departed from the pure worship of Jehovah. Jeroboam, the first king of the northern 10 tribes, established calf worship at Dan and Bethel. But calf worship at least pretended to represent the worship of Jehovah. Jezebel, through her influence on Ahab, offered a completely new departure for Israel—official worship of Baal. The Bible gives extensive coverage to Israel at its peak, under David and Solomon, and also to Israel at its depth—under Ahab. That's how we know so much about Jezebel's part in Israel's downward slide.

Ahab's father, Omri, brought calf worship to its peak. "And Omri did evil in the sight of the Lord, and acted more wickedly than all who were before him" (1 Kings 16:25). Ahab went a step further and brought in Baalism. "And Ahab the son of Omri did evil in the sight of the Lord more than all who were before him" (1 Kings 16:30). So under the influence of Jezebel, Israel reached its very lowest point religiously.

Naturally, the gaiety and low morals of Baal worship appealed to the Israelites. As you walk about the ruins of the ancient city of Samaria, you can see foundation stones of the palace, and also of the temple for the worship of Baal. Ahab "went to serve Baal and worshiped him. So he erected an altar for Baal in the house of Baal, which he built in Samaria" (1 Kings 16:31-32).

The greater part of the structure for Baal worship was a courtyard enclosed with thick walls. Within it stood a small chapel containing symbols of Baal and the mother-goddess Asherah. These represented the male and female principles of reproduction. They were designed to stimulate the sexual orgies with which the god of fertility was worshiped. Worshipers believed these orgies would encourage the gods to give fertility to field and flock.

Naturally, all the looseness of Baal worship horrified devout Israelites. But it tempted many others, with the same appeal as the "new morality" offers Christians today. The Israelite worship of a holy God looked austere by comparison.

Jezebel never wavered in her objective. She never considered the attractions of Judaism. In the age-long struggle between good and evil, Jezebel gave evil an enormous boost.

We might admire the thoroughness with which Ethbaal indoctrinated Jezebel with his beliefs. We would do well to indoctrinate our children, and to devote ourselves to the cause of Christ as thoroughly as Jezebel devoted herself to Baal.

When Jezebel seemed to have everything going her own way, Elijah appeared. God doesn't leave evil to flourish unchallenged. The most powerful of all the prophets rose up to oppose Jezebel. Elijah stood as strongly for God as Jezebel stood for Baal.

Jezebel's Methods

The Bible pronounces both Jezebel and Ahab evil. They differed only in degree. Jezebel was strong and evil. Ahab was weak and evil. Any weak person who thinks he can safely continue in his weakness will sooner or later fall into the hands of a Jezebel.

Ahab gave some thought to God, as shown by the names of some of his children: *Ahaziah,* "Jehovah supports"; *Jehoram,* "Jehovah is exalted"; *Athaliah,* "Jehovah is strong." He had appointed a God-fearing man, Obadiah, as head of his household. He trembled before Elijah, and he allowed the contest on Mount Carmel, between Elijah and the prophets of Baal, to take place. He accepted the outcome of that great victory for Jehovah—at least until he told Jezebel about it.

But Ahab was weaker than both Elijah and Jezebel, who batted him back and forth between them like a tennis ball.

Elijah appeared on the scene with dramatic suddenness, then disappeared for three years. "Now Elijah the Tishbite, who was of the settlers of Gilead, said to Ahab, 'As the Lord, the God of Israel lives, before whom I stand, surely there shall be neither dew nor rain these years, except by my word' " (1 Kings 17:1). Baal was supposed to control the forces of nature. Elijah stated that God controls rain.

It got so dry that Ahab feared he would lose all his domestic animals. He called his household overseer, Obadiah, and told him to go through all the land in search of grass. They divided the land between them, Obadiah going one way, and Ahab another, to search out all the fountains and waterbrooks in hopes of finding a little grass.

We learn from Obadiah something about Jezebel's methods. "When Jezebel destroyed the prophets of the Lord . . . Obadiah took a hundred prophets and hid them by fifties in a cave, and provided them with bread and water" (1 Kings 18:4). This called for courage in Obadiah. Jezebel sought to wipe out Jehovah worship by direct approach—ruthlessly destroying the prophets of God. She seemed to have no conscience to hold her back from the most cruel and relentless methods. Obadiah took his life in his hands to defy her order.

"Obadiah feared the Lord greatly" (1 Kings 18:3). We learn something about Ahab from his appointment of Obadiah as steward of his household. Ahab was not totally evil. His crime? He let Jezebel manipulate him for evil. Ahab would not have accomplished so much evil without the overpowering strength of Jezebel. But even though Ahab functioned as a tool of Jezebel, God still held him totally responsible. In pronouncing judgment on Ahab, God didn't excuse him for not standing up to Jezebel.

There is no excuse for us to claim, as a child does, "He made me do it." Any mother knows she must drill into her children they can't go along with someone else in wrongdoing. "Even a child is known by his doings, whether his work be pure, and whether it be right" (Prov. 20:11, KJV).

When our son Dan was about eight years of age, he learned this lesson the hard way. A policeman showed up at our door with our son in tow. The policeman informed us that Dan had been involved in starting a fire under someone's car. It turned out Dan was not actually committing the act; however, he was across the street laughing and spurring on his friend. A woman who looked out her window didn't know the kid by the car, but she knew the boy across the street—the minister's son. It proved a valuable lesson for Dan.

Differing weights of personalities create intriguing contrasts in marriages. Some men with overbearing wives maintain their own integrity by simply not talking. Their wives' words beat away at them, yet they go their own way and pay no attention. Others battle vigorously to maintain their right-of-way. Others live their own lives quite independently; but in matters concerning both of them, they simply give way. "You can't beat city hall," said one. Still others, like Ahab, abdicate their power and let themselves become tools. Anything to keep the peace. Jezebel moved with relentless ferocity toward her goals.

"Now it came about after many days, that the word of the Lord came to Elijah in the third year, saying, 'Go, show yourself to Ahab, and I will send rain on the face of the earth.' So Elijah went to show himself to Ahab. Now the famine was severe in Samaria" (1 Kings 18:1-2).

God had sought to speak to Ahab and Jezebel through *prosperity*. Ahab's father, Omri, had bought the hill of Samaria which rose 300 feet from the mountain valley around it. For the six years Omri reigned he must have worked constantly on constructing buildings on the hill. His son Ahab continued the building activities and then moved in.

The Bible refers to the ivory house which Ahab made (1 Kings 22:39). It sounded like legend, but when archeologists excavated, they found the house. The foundations of Samaria rested on virgin soil. Sure enough, Omri had in fact acquired new land. Huge blocks forming the strong fortifications show the plan—outer walls 15 feet thick surrounding a wide courtyard, in which was the royal palace. And the diggers noticed something very unusual. Innumerable fragments of ivory were discovered in every square yard of the excavation. For Omri and Ahab had in fact built a house with walls adorned with ivory and containing furniture made of or decorated with ivory.

In Samaria Jezebel enjoyed many of the luxuries she knew in Sidon. But prosperity didn't speak to her or to Ahab of God.

Now God sent *adversity*—a drought. As three and one-half long years wore away, Jezebel in her ivory house must have longed for refreshing rain. All the wild orgies to Baal requesting rain, and all the human sacrifices to him availed nothing. The drought turned into famine. And where was Elijah? Nobody could find him. Ahab and Jezebel blamed him for the drought. If only they could find Elijah, they could vent their bitterness on him.

One day Elijah appeared to Obadiah and told the steward to send Ahab to him. That King Ahab answered the summons shows the awe the prophet inspired.

Jezebel was away from Samaria at the time, at their winter home in Jezreel (1 Kings 18:45-46). Ahab greeted Elijah as "you troubler of Israel" (1 Kings 18:17). Elijah answered, "I have not troubled Israel, but you and your father's house have, because you have forsaken the commandments of the Lord, and you have followed the Baals" (1 Kings 18:18).

Elijah then summoned Ahab to the great contest on Mount Carmel. "Now then send and gather to me all Israel at Mount Carmel, together with 450 prophets of Baal and 400 prophets of the Asherah, who eat at Jezebel's table" (1 Kings 18:19). Ahab gathered them all together on Mount Carmel, which looms between the territory of Sidon, and that of Israel.

The contest between Elijah and the priests resulted in a magnificent triumph for Jehovah. The 850 prophets of Baal and Ashtoreth danced like dervishes, crying to their gods hour after hour. Elijah, representing Jehovah, stood alone against them.

Elijah spoke quietly to God; and immediately fire came down from heaven to burn his sacrifice. Then came the longed-for rainstorm. Jehovah had completely bested Baal, the supposed god of fertility. For Jehovah alone controls the forces of nature.

For a little while, until he saw Jezebel, Ahab believed. "And when all the people saw it, they fell on their faces; and they said, 'The Lord, He is God'" (1 Kings 18:39). Ahab allowed Elijah to order the people to slay the prophets of Baal—those murderers of little children. It was a fight to the death. Jezebel had already killed off most of the prophets of the Lord.

"The sky grew black with clouds and wind, and there was a heavy shower" (18:45). Surely all this would convince Jezebel! "And Ahab rode and went to Jezreel. Then the hand of the Lord was on Elijah, and he girded up his loins and outran Ahab to Jezreel" (1 Kings 18:45-46).

Elijah, exhilarated by the events of the day, ran before the chariot of Ahab. He must have felt certain that Jezebel would accept what worked. No doubt he believed the day was won; Jezebel as well as Ahab would be impressed.

"Now Ahab told Jezebel all that Elijah had done, and how he had killed all the prophets with the sword" (19:1). Jezebel was not impressed. She only heard that the prophets of Baal had perished. Nothing could convince Jezebel. She, like some people today might say, "Don't confuse me with the facts. My mind is made up."

"Then Jezebel sent a messenger to Elijah, saying, 'So may the gods do to me and even more, if I do not make your life as the life of one of them by tomorrow about this time'" (19:2).

Elijah had stood up to Ahab, he'd stood up to 850 prophets in their noisy and grotesque worship. He'd stood up to all Israel. But this message from Jezebel made him turn and run (19:3).

The next picture of Ahab and Jezebel together gives us an episode from their domestic life. Her method of controlling Ahab was to appeal to his lowest and most selfish instincts.

"Now it came about after these things, that Naboth the Jezreel-ite had a vineyard which was in Jezreel beside the palace of Ahab king of Samaria" (21:1). Like all the rest of us, Ahab could always think of one thing more to round out his possessions. He looked out the window of his winter palace in Jezreel and saw a plot of ground he wanted for a garden. He said to Naboth, "Give me your vineyard, that I may have it for a vegetable garden because it is close beside my house, and I will give you a better vineyard than it in its place; if you like, I will give you the price of it in money" (21:2).

Ahab was comparatively mild-mannered. He made what he felt was a more than fair offer for the plot of ground. The owner, Naboth, refused. "The Lord forbid me that I should give you the inheritance of my fathers" (21:3). God ordained in the Law of Moses that property was not to collect in the hands of kings and wealthy people. It was to pass down through families.

King Ahab knew that Naboth was well within his rights in refusing him, and he evidently would have dropped the matter.

But he was disappointed. "Ahab came into his house sullen and vexed. . . . And he lay down on his bed and turned away his face and ate no food" (21:4). He could have been lying on the couch on which Orientals reclined at mealtime. Or it could have been a bed in his own room. Ordinary people slept on mats on the floor, but very wealthy people did have beds. Either way, we see the picture of a pouting king. Jezebel came around to find out what was wrong, as we all feel compelled to do when someone pouts.

"How is it that your spirit is so sullen that you are not eating food?" (21:5) Jezebel asked. Ahab told her he had offered Naboth money or another piece of land for his vineyard, and that Naboth had refused.

So Jezebel taunted him, "Do you now reign over Israel? Arise, eat bread, and let your heart be joyful; I will give you the vineyard of Naboth the Jezreelite" (21:7).

Jezebel thought in terms of the absolute monarchy of Tyre, where the king's whim was law. Ahab understood a king of Israel was to be limited by God's Law. But he offered no objections when Jezebel said she would get him the vineyard. Nothing moves a weak man so much as the fear of being thought weak.

Suppose you wanted a new car, and knew you couldn't possibly afford it. But you sulked and pouted for that car until your husband said, "Don't worry, I'll get a car for you." You certainly would want to know whether he was going to beg, borrow, or steal it. But not Ahab. He asked no questions of Jezebel. And he certainly knew her ruthlessness.

Jezebel whizzed into action. She wrote letters in Ahab's name, sealed them with his seal, and sent them to elders and nobles in Jezreel. She knew the Law of God well enough to make a mockery of it to trap Naboth. She was not only evil, but also very clever. She followed the law while mocking its deepest intention.

First she called for a public fast. That meant that someone had sinned and that the Israelites must meet in solemn assembly to confess their sin to God, and root out whatever sin was in their midst. She arranged for Naboth to be set in a prominent place at the fast. Two false witnesses should be seated opposite him. They were to testify that he had cursed both God and the king. Then would follow the due penalty of the law (Deut. 24:16). Naboth would be taken out of the city and stoned to death. We learn later that his sons were also stoned at this time (2 Kings 9:26). Once no living descendants existed to inherit the property, it would automatically revert to the king.

Any number of dictators throughout history have done the same things—killed and then seized the property of their subjects. Israel had sunk to the level of the nations around it. Or lower—even using the Law of God for destructive ends.

Those elders and nobles abdicated responsibility for their own acts. Not one of them said, "Naboth is one of us. This is wrong. We cannot follow such a directive." Throughout the Scriptures, we see the principle that we are responsible. "We must obey God rather than men" (Acts 5:29).

Jezebel's personality struck fear to the hearts of everyone. Elijah fled for his life at receiving her message. Her husband put himself in her hands. The elders and nobles obeyed her instructions without question. Think of what she could have accomplished if she had used such force of personality for good!

Presently, the elders sent word that Naboth had died by stoning. "Jezebel said to Ahab, 'Arise, take possession of the vineyard of Naboth, the Jezreelite, which he refused to give you for money; for Naboth is not alive, but dead'" (1 Kings 21:15). Notice Ahab never inquired as to what happened to Naboth. He was quite willing to receive the benefits of her act. He seemed to feel that not knowing the facts meant he was not a party to whatever had taken place.

"Ahab arose to go down to the vineyard of Naboth the Jezreelite, to take possession of it" (21:16). Ahab went to inspect his new toy. No doubt he had wonderful plans for it. He was already tasting the vegetables and fruits that would grow in his garden.

Jezebel's Results

Ahab's pleasure proved short-lived. Jezebel's objectives and methods were soon to produce their inevitable results. At that very moment God was telling Elijah to meet Ahab in the vineyard.

Elijah's message for Ahab: "Thus says the Lord, 'Have you murdered, and also taken possession? . . . In the place where the dogs licked up the blood of Naboth the dogs shall lick up your blood, even yours!'" (21:19)

Ahab let Jezebel convince him that he was above the law. Yet the very sight of Elijah spoke to Ahab before the prophet ever opened his mouth. Have you ever felt your presence was an unwelcome rebuke to someone, whether you said anything or not?

We've all felt the wordless rebuke of parents. Once my mother made some fudge and left it to cool. My sister and I took it and ran off to a closet. We were digging into it with spoons when my mother opened the door and silently looked at us. Nothing could have made us feel more guilty.

Upon seeing Elijah Ahab said, "Hast thou found me, O mine enemy?" (1 Kings 21:20) Elijah only *seemed* like an enemy to Ahab. He really wanted the highest good for Ahab, for Jezebel, and for the kingdom of Israel. Had they listened, they could have saved themselves from suffering and disgrace. We too may cut ourselves off from valuable criticism by viewing the critic as an enemy.

"I have found you, because you have sold yourself to do evil in the sight of the Lord" (21:20). The Hebrew word *maker* means literally to sell as merchandise, as a daughter into marriage, or as a slave into bondage. Figuratively, it means to surrender. Ahab had given himself over to evil.

No doubt Jezebel fancied she had succeeded. But God always has the last word, and ultimate results lie with Him. Ahab and all his male descendants would be cut off. For Jezebel, Elijah pronounced a wretched end. "The dogs shall eat Jezebel in the district of Jezreel" (21:23).

The writer of 1 Kings then summarized the life of Ahab and his relationship to Jezebel. "Surely there was no one like Ahab who sold himself to do evil in the sight of the Lord, because Jezebel his wife incited him. And he acted very abominably in following idols, according to all that the Amorites had done whom the Lord cast out before the sons of Israel" (21:25-26).

Ahab got the point. He humbled himself before God, put on the outward signs of mourning—tore his clothes, wore scratchy sack-cloth, fasted, lay in sackcloth, "and went about despondently" (21:27). A loving parent snatches at straws of encouragement that a child is going to do better. So does our loving heavenly Father. "Because he has humbled himself before Me, I will not bring the evil in his days, but I will bring the evil upon his house in his son's days" (21:29).

Jezebel lived to see the death of her husband and the murder of her sons, before her own violent end. Ahab died in battle, and was brought back to Samaria. The dogs licked up his blood as servants washed his chariot in the pool of Samaria. Archeologists have found a large artificial basin in the courtyard of Ahab's palace, which is thought to be the pool in which Ahab's blood was washed off his chariot.

Ahab's son Ahaziah, well trained in the school of evil, reigned over Israel in Samaria for two years. "And he did evil in the sight of the Lord and walked in the way of his father and in the way of his mother" (22:52). We might say that Ahab and Jezebel succeeded as parents. This oldest son, heir to the throne, shared their values completely. He carried on their objectives and methods.

We can learn even from Ahab and Jezebel. They were very positive, very committed, very consistent. Ahab wavered a little, but Jezebel didn't waver at all in her dedication to evil. Both father and mother made their impression upon Ahaziah. But after only two years of reigning, Ahaziah died from an accident—he fell down through a lattice in an upper room.

Then another son of Ahab came to the throne of Israel—Jehoram. "And he did evil in the sight of the Lord, though not like his father and like his mother; for he put away the sacred pillar of Baal which his father had made. Nevertheless, he clung to the sins of Jeroboam the son of Nebat, which he made Israel sin; he did not depart from it" (2 Kings 3:2-3).

Jehoram stepped back from actively promoting Baal worship in Israel. But he still adhered to the false worship of Jehovah—the calf worship which Jeroboam, first king after Solomon, had established. During those years Jezebel exercised control as queen mother of Israel. She also influenced the southern kingdom of Judah for the worse when her daughter Athaliah married Jehoram, king of Judah. This descendant of David ruling the Southern Kingdom "walked in the way of the kings of Israel, just as the house of Ahab had done, for the daughter of Ahab became his wife; and he did evil in the sight of the Lord" (2 Kings 8:18). Jezebel exerted her evil influence through her husband, and through her children.

In the end, Jezebel found her life turning to ashes. The gaiety that she thought she had brought to Israel didn't exist. The king of Syria came up and besieged Samaria, till famine became so terrible that a woman boiled and ate her own son (2 Kings 6:28-29).

God tried everything to get through to Jezebel. No doubt He saw great possibilities in her powerful personality. He sent her prosperity, then adversity. He allowed her to be queen of his chosen nation. He sent two of His greatest prophets, and a whole cluster of miracles. There had been few miracles since God had freed Israel from Egypt. There would not be so many again until the captivity in Babylon, nor again till the time of Christ's ministry, and the beginning of the church.

In how many different ways has God tried to speak to you? Have you heard Him? Nothing got through to Jezebel. In the end, God called Jehu to execute judgment: "You shall strike the house of Ahab your master, that I may avenge the blood of My servants the prophets, and the blood of all the servants of the Lord, at the hand of Jezebel. For the whole house of Ahab shall perish. . . . And the dogs shall eat Jezebel in the territory of Jezreel, and none shall bury her" (2 Kings 9:7-10).

King Joram, Jezebel's son, met Jehu outside the city of Jezreel. The remains of the city stand today on a spur of Mount Gilboa, at the eastern end of the great valley of Jezreel. "Is it peace, Jehu?" asked Joram.

Jehu answered, "What peace, so long as the harlotries of your mother Jezebel and her witchcrafts are so many?" (9:22) Jezebel continued to exert her influence as queen mother.

When Jezebel received news that Jehu had shot Joram through the heart with an arrow, she reacted strangely. She knew she would die next at Jehu's hands. "And she painted her eyes and adorned her head, and looked out the window" (2 Kings 9:30).

In the ruins of Ahab's ivory house, archeologists have found small stone boxes for mixing cosmetics. A number of small holes in these contained the various colors: kohl for black; turquoise for green; ocher for red. There was a central depression for mixing. Traces of red could still be seen.

Proud and defiant to the end, Jezebel, dressed like a queen, sat in the window of her palace as if she were greeting guests, and taunted Jehu. "Had Zimri peace, who slew his master?" Jehu knew as well as she did that Zimri gained the throne by violence, but reigned for only seven days.

Jehu looked up toward the window and shouted, "Who is on my side? Who?" Two eunuchs looked out, and Jehu ordered, "Throw her down." So they threw her down. Jezebel had not won the love of her servants. She died from the fall onto the stone courtyard, and was trodden by the horses.

Jehu was allowed immediate entrance into the royal villa, and was served a banquet. After he had eaten and drunk, he ordered, "See now to this cursed woman and bury her, for she is a king's daughter" (2 Kings 9:34).

But the dreadful prophecy of Elijah had come true. "And they went to bury her, but they found no more of her than the skull and the feet and the palms of her hands" (2 Kings 9:35). Wild scavenger dogs that roamed about ancient cities of the Middle East had dragged off and devoured her body.

Jehu's final words to King Joram sum up the tragedy of Jezebel's life: "What peace, so long as the harlotries of your mother Jezebel and her witchcrafts are so many?" (2 Kings 9:22) At the end he called her "this cursed woman" (2 Kings 9:34)—one who had brought God's curse upon herself.

Jezebel was a woman of intelligence, glamour, and attractiveness. She was a king's daughter and then a queen, with every advantage. Yet she devoted her life to the wrong objective. She shut God out, and refused all His pleas. She corrupted a nation, destroyed her family, and destroyed herself.

She, like every one of us, held in her hands her greatest

power—the power of choice. And her life proved the principle expressed so many years later by the Apostle Paul: "Do not be deceived, God is not mocked; for whatever a man sows, this he will also reap" (Gal. 6:7).

10
How to Work
with Your Husband

In the pages of the New Testament we come upon a marriage as modern as tomorrow's newspaper, but as old as the Christian faith. We find Priscilla and Aquila together in business, together in Christ, together in travel, together in their service of hospitality and teaching. They took risks together and suffered together. They represent the modern egalitarian marriage.

In the 1950s, when women were trying so hard to "find" themselves as total housewives and mothers, one writer said: "The solution for the woman who wants something more than babies and household chores is to marry a farmer or a minister. When she marries her husband, she marries a career."

Today, although many husbands and wives seek separate careers, there are others who find fulfillment in togetherness. John and Cheri carry on a basement waterproofing business from their home. Says Cheri, "Being involved with my husband in business sometimes is hectic, but I feel I am using my God-given abilities. When I get the children into bed and go downstairs to work in our basement office for a few hours, I feel refreshed and challenged. I know I have a good head for business. Being involved means my husband listens to me and is interested in what I have to say."

Jerry and Sharon work together professionally in music. He directs the church choirs and teaches. She accompanies and gives private lessons at home. They perform together.

"Besides improving our marriage, working together in music

makes for a better outcome," says Jerry. "Our strengths and weaknesses are complementary. She fills in where I might miss."

Many partners in marriage feel they have reached their God-given potential as individuals through working together as a team. While some husbands and wives cancel each other out by pulling in different directions, others grow through identifying.

Together in Business

After Paul left Athens, he went to Corinth. He left the center of learning to go to the center of commerce and vice. Does it seem strange that he considered that center of materialism and sensu--ality an ideal place for spreading the Gospel?

Corinth was located on the narrow isthmus of land connecting northern with southern Greece. All overland travel from north to south went through Corinth. And much sea shipping was transported over that five-mile-wide isthmus, because travel around the southern tip of Greece meant a 200-mile trip. It also meant facing severe dangers of shipwreck, because of rocks jutting out into the Mediterranean and stormy conditions at that point. So Corinth developed as a crossroads.

Corinth became a center of vice, a sailors' town where the lid was off. Its temple to Aphrodite, located high on the Acrocorinthus above the town, glorified physical love and encouraged lust. One thousand temple priestesses plied their trade of sacred prostitution.

As Paul walked into a city famous throughout the Roman world for debauchery, he may have felt overwhelmed. The temple to Venus or Aphrodite, goddess of love, dominated the city geographically and socially. Imagine his feelings as he wondered how he could work for Christ in such a place. Yet Paul believed that whatever God called him to do, He would make possible, step by step.

For Paul the first step in that strange and rough city was earning a living. Though he was by formal education a rabbi, he was also trained in a trade, as were all rabbis in that day. So he sought out the section of the marketplace where tentmakers made and sold their wares. He found Priscilla and Aquila working away at their task of weaving the black goats-hair cloth, then cutting and sewing the parts of a tent together. They had recently come from Rome, and they invited Paul to work with them, using their equipment. (See Acts 18:2-3.)

Cheri had worked in business before she married John. Sharon and Jerry had worked together in music for three years before they even had a date.

Says Jerry, "From our first encounter, we shared a strong common interest. Just out of college, I taught music in a high school. After tryouts, I selected Sharon as accompanist for the choir. I saw her as a very talented young lady. Through working together, we built mutual respect. Mutual respect led to admiration that grew into love. She graduated and went away to college. We actually had only three dates before we became engaged. However, those dates extended over a period of time during which we exchanged many letters and talked on the phone. Of course, we knew each other from the long association of working together.

"Ours has been a partnership that grows. Our marriage is built on doing things together as a team. On vacation, we often perform together. When I came to my present position as director of music in the church, I was hired and Sharon came along as my wife. Subsequently, she was hired as accompanist."

Says John, "There are many advantages to having your wife in business with you. In getting established, it helps a lot because you don't have to pay that extra salary. Also, one person's weakness is another person's strength. I tend to have the business viewpoint—what's needed to make the business go. Cheri usually has the viewpoint of the customer. Through working with me, Cheri gains more sensitivity to problems of the business, more understanding of what I'm up against.

"Whether it works out or not depends on the relationship. It is necessary to look on it as a team effort—not as boss and employee. As a team, you each know your own job and do it. With your mate, it's pretty hard to put the pressure on and demand that a thing be done at a certain time. She has her own ideas of how she wants to spend her time. But when she carries responsibility, she brings things together as necessary."

Says Cheri, "Working with your husband means a real step forward in communication. Men like to talk about politics, work, and sports. Women like to talk about things having to do with the house and the children. When I know what my husband is doing professionally, we can always discuss business. I can give suggestions. He makes the final decision, because he has to live with it. But he needs my perspective. He's not as atune as I am to the details of consumer opinion.

"A man may get bored when a woman talks about the house or the children. He listens politely, smiles occasionally. But when we talk about business, it's one to one, he looks me right in the eye, is very serious with me, talks to me as an adult. I feel appreciated, important. I think it's very healthy. I know I'm contributing something.

"I take care of the customers on the phone. I also advise the workmen when they call in panicking because something has gone wrong. I can't advise them technically, but I can discuss the problem from the common sense point of view, and advise what to do. I do the banking and part of the bookkeeping, send letters and write checks. The telephone answering is constant, 20 to 30 calls a day. It's all something completely different from housework and children. I enjoy it because it gives me a larger horizon."

Together in Christ

While Paul stayed with Priscilla and Aquila, "he was reasoning in the synagogue every Sabbath and trying to persuade Jews and Greeks" (Acts 18:4). We can picture the three in the tent shop, working away with their hands, and talking together. Paul must have shared with them hour after hour from the depths of his great soul. His words took root, grew, and blossomed in the lives of Aquila and Priscilla. Many a modern worker in office, factory, or school has shared Christ with fellow workers, teachers, or students. We see great results from such sharing.

"When Silas and Timothy came down from Macedonia, Paul began devoting himself completely to the Word, solemnly testifying to the Jews that Jesus was the Christ" (18:5). Apparently, Silas and Timothy brought support money to Paul from the Philippian church, so that Paul became free to devote his entire time to preaching and teaching. But he had permanently affected the lives of Priscilla and Aquila through his brief time of working with them. They now became his co-workers in Christ.

Says Jerry, "When I was first working with Sharon in music, I learned she was a believer. After that our relationship deepened. In our work now together, I have the broader background in music, more training. My viewpoint is to enhance worship with good music. I always want to put on a good musical performance. Sharon constantly emphasizes our mutual sense of mission through music. Our ministry is a combination of both of us."

Says Cheri, "It means so much in business to be together in the Lord. Maybe one of us is worried, and is taking it out on the other one. The other one can say to stop right there, to resign from worry. We can talk over the problem, pray about it, then leave it with the Lord.

"John and I together attend two home Bible study groups. We both enjoy this. In the free and open discussions, we can see where our partner stands on subjects we don't talk about ordinarily. Then we can try to understand and accept the other's viewpoint. For example, to me faith comes easily. John says I have a blind faith. He has to ask questions, think more rationally.

"But when he's worried, he opens up with his concerns, and asks me to pray about the problems. Our marriage is growing all the time. Several couples have told us they think we're one of the happiest couples they know."

Together in Travel

After a year and a half of working with Jews and Gentiles in Corinth, Paul took his leave and sailed for Syria. Priscilla and Aquila went along as far as Ephesus.

We see Aquila and Priscilla as a pair who moved a lot, as many families do today. Aquila, a Jew, was born in Pontus, a Roman province of northern Asia Minor. Jews were dispersed throughout the ancient world. Jews from Pontus were in Jerusalem on that great day of Pentecost, and heard the Galileans speak in the native tongue of Pontus (Acts 2:7-9). Peter addressed his first letter "to those who reside as aliens, scattered throughout Pontus," and other provinces of Asia Minor (1 Peter 1:1).

Perhaps because Pontus was a Roman province, Aquila went to Rome to seek his fortune. There he set up shop as a tentmaker, and there he met Priscilla. Some speculate that she came from a noble family in Rome. Or she may have been a freedwoman bearing the name of that Roman family. At any rate she met and married the Jewish tentmaker. Maybe they both had some contact with Christianity in Rome. There were also Jewish visitors from Rome at that first Pentecost in Jerusalem (Acts 2:10). From Paul's letter, we know that a group of Christians existed in Rome before Paul arrived there.

Priscilla and Aquila had to leave Rome because Claudius banished all Jews in A.D. 49. The Jews were often objects of persecution in Rome. This particular occasion was probably that mentioned by Suetonius (*Life of Claudius* xxv. 4): "As the Jews were indulging in constant riots at the instigation of Chrestus, [Claudius] banished them from Rome." Perhaps these were disorders arising from the introduction of Christianity into the Roman Jewish community. The authorities, of course, didn't distinguish between Christians and Jews.

After meeting Paul in Corinth, Priscilla and Aquila became definitely rooted in something other than a city—the church. They probably found it not too difficult to move from Corinth to Ephesus, because they wanted to go with Paul. At Ephesus they evidently found good opportunities for business and for the Gospel. Ephesus served as center for the whole region. Perhaps they and Paul had already shared a vision for planting the Gospel there. Paul made a beginning before moving on to Syria, and Priscilla and Aquila stayed to carry on the work. Later Paul returned to Ephesus and did what some consider his greatest work.

Aquila and Priscilla still lived in Ephesus when Paul returned and wrote to the Corinthians. In his first letter to the Corinthian church he wrote, "The churches of Asia greet you. Aquila and Prisca greet you heartily in the Lord, with the church that is in their house" (1 Cor. 16:19).

Later, they seem to be in Rome—perhaps due to relaxed restrictions of the Jews following Claudius' death. "Greet Prisca and Aquila my fellow workers in Christ Jesus," wrote Paul in his letter to the Romans (16:3).

Still later, they were back in Ephesus. When Paul wrote his very last letter, from the dungeon in Rome, he sent only two messages to friends. One of these he directed to this couple: "Greet Prisca and Aquila" (2 Tim. 4:19). Paul characteristically used her formal Greek name, Prisca, while Luke in writing the Book of Acts, used the diminutive form, Priscilla.

If Priscilla wasn't Jewish, she could have resented having to leave Rome because her husband was. But she, like many wives and husbands since, totally identified. His lot was her lot in life. Many wives today don't enjoy being transferred from city to city because of their husbands' work. But through love for their partners, they make the change. Being together in the same work certainly makes such moves easier. Couples engaged in separate careers face an enormous problem when one wants to make a move. If the Lord comes first in both lives, the decision of where and when to move becomes much easier.

Priscilla would have missed her claim to greatness had she refused to leave Rome. She would have missed going down in history as a great force in the early church. Tertullian, early Christian writer, recorded, "By the holy Prisca, the Gospel is preached." One of the oldest catacombs of Rome, the Coemeterium Priscilla, was named in her honor. A church, "Titulus St. Prisca," was built on the Aventine hill in Rome. It bore the inscription "Titulus Aquila et Prisca." The name *Prisca* appears often on monuments of Rome.

Most women today move to a new location graciously, if reluctantly, and find new outlets, new opportunities for the Gospel wherever they go. Joan hated to leave her Bible class and her church in a suburb of Detroit. She had to go when her husband's company transferred him. But in Port Huron she found doors open for the Gospel through her witness.

My husband and his sister grew up with a great sense of security, though they never lived in one place more than 18 months. In their evangelistic ministry, his parents moved from place to place. The children found their security, not in location, but in family and the Lord. Children—and adults—can stand an amazing amount of change if they find consistency of faith and trust in their lives. Frequent changes need not knock families and individuals to pieces. Priscilla and Aquila apparently had no trouble in agreeing when a move represented God's will for them. They were ready to go when their change of location could further the Gospel.

Together in Service

Priscilla and Aquila served God by moving when opportunity beckoned. Paul spoke of them as "my fellow workers in Christ Jesus" (Rom. 16:3). The Greek word used here is *sunergos,* "a companion in labor, fellow helper, a laborer together with." From it we get our word *synergy,* which means "a combined action or operation."

Priscilla and Aquila also served God by putting down roots and settling in. In Corinth they lived in a house big enough to take in Paul as a boarder. In Ephesus they took Apollos "unto them," perhaps into their home, for instruction in the Gospel. When Paul sent greetings to the Corinthians from Aquila and Priscilla at Ephesus, he also sent greetings from the church that met in their house (1 Cor. 16:19). Later on, when Paul sent greetings from Corinth to Priscilla and Aquila at Rome, he also greeted the church that was in their house, this time in Rome. They opened their home to seekers and inquirers, as well as for meetings.

Although Priscilla and Aquila apparently had no children, they maintained a good-sized home. No church buildings existed until the third century, though synagogues were common. All Christian groups met in homes where a large enough room afforded space for them to gather.

Priscilla and Aquila gave of their home. In so doing they enlarged their own world and became known throughout the early church. It took two to engage in such a sharing. For either one could have said, "Our home is for us," and cancelled out their great ministry of hospitality.

Today, though we enjoy the use of ample church buildings,

nothing takes the place of the church in the home. Home Bible studies can include people who won't go to a church, and give opportunity for members of the body of Christ from different denominations to get together.

Through entertaining, you can build friendships with non-Christians and share your own faith in Christ as Saviour. You can open your home as you take in people who are in trouble, helping them to get on their feet. Several couples I know have bought houses and equipment for accommodating 40 or 50 people. They entertain church groups, open their homes to young people, and hold Bible studies.

Priscilla and Aquila also functioned together in ministry as teachers. "Now a certain Jew named Apollos, an Alexandrian by birth, an eloquent man, came to Ephesus; and he was mighty in the Scriptures. This man had been instructed in the way of the Lord; and being fervent in spirit, he was speaking and teaching accurately the things concerning Jesus, being acquainted only with the baptism of John; and he began to speak out boldly in the synagogue. But when Priscilla and Aquila heard him, they took him aside and explained to him the way of God more accurately" (Acts 18:24-26).

Coming from Alexandria, Apollos probably had very thorough grounding in the Old Testament Scriptures. Alexandria was an Egyptian university center, preeminent for learning in the ancient world, along with Athens and Tarsus. It was also a great center for Jews. Two of the five wards of the city were Jewish. The Septuagint translation of the Old Testament into Greek came out of Alexandria, several centuries before Christ.

Furthermore, Apollos was a natural orator. But Aquila and Priscilla knew something he didn't—they knew Christ. Humbly and tactfully they shared what they had. We can imagine how they might have begun by commending Apollos for what he did know, and for his skill and natural talent in speaking. They saw him not as a person who was preaching the wrong message, but as a potentially great power for Christ. Because they accepted him where he was in his spiritual life, they could gently and wisely lead him on to a full knowledge of Christ. Paul's teaching of Priscilla and Aquila had not been in vain. Now that Paul had moved on to Jerusalem and Antioch, they could instruct the gifted Apollos.

We marvel at Apollos' maturity and wisdom in accepting instruction from members of his congregation. Unlike a lot of people, he was willing to learn. Eventually, Apollos moved on to Corinth, warmly commended by the believers in Ephesus. Thanks to the efforts of Aquila and Priscilla, he became a great influence in the Corinthian church.

Who was the leader in the partnership of Aquila and Priscilla? We don't know. Priscilla's name comes first in four out of the six times they're mentioned in Scripture. Some say she was mentioned first because of her social position. However, most commentators feel she was mentioned first because she was a strong and able person, one who carried real influence in the early church. But she and her husband worked together, each rejoicing in the other's abilities.

Says Jerry, "I had to come to terms with the fact that Sharon has more of a natural ear for music than I do. Mine is a trained ear. When someone hums a tune and wants me to play it, I turn the request over to Sharon. Or when someone wants a song transposed into a different key, I can do it by thinking it through theoretically. Sharon can sit down and play it by ear. I learned that her strengths are my strengths. When I'm directing a choir, she often hears something that's not just right. Either she plays the weak spot on the piano, or whispers to me as I direct. She picks up the voids for me.

"At the present time, I'm helping her some on the organ, because she's needed as assistant organist. We complement each other."

Says Sharon, "When we were first married, I had some tough adjustments to make. We went to summer conferences where I had previously been the whole show musically, playing both piano and organ. Now Jerry plays the organ, because he's a better organist than I am. I learned not to feel jealous—because he is part of me.

"It's so wonderful to be in this work together, and it's important to serve Christ through my music. I would be left home alone so many nights if we weren't performing together. But when we're both involved, and both responsible, the children understand. They expect me to go when Daddy goes. These nights when we are out together performing or working with the choirs are like dates, things that we do together. And I'm growing all the time. Jerry keeps before me things he wants me to do, ways in which he wants me to grow. I work very hard to please him and try to do whatever he thinks I can do.

"When we first met, he as teacher was the great master in charge. When we got married we sometimes found ourselves in a tug of war. It could have been bad. But I am really happy as the accompanist. I really don't want to be up front. He has more training for being in charge. I enjoy helping. Because of working so closely together, we're closer in our marriage, and we're best friends. There's always so much to talk about. We think, plan, discuss everything together."

As Priscilla and Aquila worked together, moved about, and committed their lives to Christ, they took risks. Paul wrote of Priscilla and Aquila ". . . who for my life risked their own necks, to whom not only do I give thanks, but also all the churches of the Gentiles" (Rom. 16:4).

Any couple who move from one place to another, travel, engage in business, and commit themselves to Christ take risks. Some couples have canceled each other out by refusing to take risks. Sometimes a husband or a wife is afraid to travel, or doesn't want to leave the comforts of home. So neither goes. One may be afraid to let her partner risk leaving the security of a dull job. So he never experiences his potential for joy and success in a job that represents self-realization. Or one is afraid to let go of his partner for the Lord's work—afraid that the Lord might come first. So they miss the togetherness of putting the Lord first in both lives.

We don't know just how Priscilla and Aquila "risked their own necks" for Paul's life. Perhaps his life was threatened in some of the rioting in Ephesus or Corinth, and they offered to take his place. Perhaps they jeopardized their own lives by taking him into their home, or by helping him to escape a dangerous situation. We don't know. At any rate, they put their lives on the line for Paul.

He thanked them, and so did the whole church. They risked life, health, and livelihood for the Gospel and they did it together. Many couples have grown immeasurably closer through risking and suffering together.

Priscilla and Aquila have come down to us as one pattern for God's ideal in marriage. Historically, the man has been emphasized as the head, with all attending advantages. Today too often feminism seeks to put the woman in the place of advantage. In Priscilla and Aquila we see an example of a marriage where neither lords it over the other.

Multitudes of couples enjoy this same kind of freedom in togetherness. As each puts the other first, both can express themselves and grow without being inhibited in any way. The sexes don't have to pit themselves against each other. The man shouldn't have to struggle for headship, nor the woman for her "rights." Too often the sexes see each other as adversaries. God created two sexes for beautiful togetherness.

My husband and I have followed the pattern of Aquila and Priscilla. We feel we have realized our potential as individuals, and plumbed the depths of love in togetherness.

11
How to Cope with Jealousy

"Everyone experiences jealousy at one time or another," says Aileen, a nurse. "You always look at the person on the next level above you—not at someone far above, or far below. You may envy someone on the same level for fancied advantages. When we had no children, we envied couples who produced one baby after another. Later when we got into all those problems with our children, we envied people who had no children!

"Envy can be good or bad. It's good if it spurs you on to qualify for more responsibility—to get that degree, to learn those techniques. It's bad if it destroys relationships."

Miriam, the sister of Moses, assumed unusual responsibility at an early age. She rose to high position, but became jealous for more power. Miriam depicts a very modern tension. We want freedom to express ourselves. We also want to maintain our relationships. The struggles of Miriam suggest ways to find self-expression within the framework of relating to other people.

We'll look at Miriam as a girl watching over the baby Moses; as a gifted woman, a prophetess, leading her people in celebration of triumph; and as a leader, second only to Moses, but jealous of him.

Miriam Watching
The Israelites came down to Egypt for bread when Joseph held great power. In four centuries they multiplied till they "became

exceedingly mighty, so that the land was filled with them" (Ex. 1:7). In the time of Joseph, Pharaoh had given them the choicest portion of the land. Then circumstances changed. "Now a new king arose over Egypt, who did not know Joseph" (Ex. 1:8). The new king feared that the Children of Israel would outnumber the Egyptians and side with their enemies in time of war. So he embarked on a program of racial persecution.

First, he afflicted the Israelites with hard labor. Today in Egypt you can see great temples and monuments which are thought to have been built by the slave labor of Israelites. But hard work didn't destroy them. To the king's dismay, they thrived under it and multiplied even more.

So the king of Egypt tried another tactic to decrease their numbers. He ordered Hebrew midwives to kill all the boy babies born to Hebrew women. "But the midwives feared God, and did not do as the king of Egypt had commanded them, but let the boys live" (Ex. 1:17).

So Pharaoh tried something else. He ordered all boy babies "cast into the Nile" (Ex. 1:22)—the great Nile that comes out of the mountains in central Africa and flows through Egypt. The river meant life to the land, creating a path of green out of the desert wastes. Pharaoh decreed it should mean death to the Hebrew race. Females could marry into Egyptian families and become absorbed. With the males dead, Hebrews as a race would cease to exist.

God, however, planned otherwise. While the adult power of a mighty nation hurled itself against those tiny infants, God worked out a plan of survival for the race, through women. First through the midwives, who refused to follow Pharaoh's decree. Then through Jochebed, Miriam, and the Pharaoh's own daughter. All these worked together in the mystery of God's providence to save the baby Moses. God even arranged that the future deliverer of the Israelites would grow up in Pharaoh's palace, and enjoy all the advantages of royal education. That education would equip him to contend with another Pharaoh later on.

But Pharaoh's plan failed. "Now a man from the house of Levi went and married a daughter of Levi. And the woman conceived and bore a son; and when she saw that he was beautiful, she hid him for three months" (Ex. 2:1-2). We can imagine that mother's anguish. Mothers love ugly children, and even misshapen or retarded children. But here was a beautiful child with all his faculties intact, one who inspired his parents to believe he had a very special future. And the law said they must expose him—cast him into the Nile to die. They didn't do it. Centuries before Peter spoke the words, they knew, "We must obey God rather than men" (Acts 5:29).

We can picture that little household of Amram and Jochebed, both descendants of Levi. All eyes must have focused on the baby Moses. Aaron had been born before the decree came into effect. They didn't have to worry about whatever noise he made. But they had to keep the tiny baby absolutely quiet. The older sister Miriam probably served as mother's right-hand helper to keep the baby from crying.

Already, Miriam was learning her lifelong role—playing second violin to Moses in the orchestra of life. For those three months the whole household subordinated feelings and interests, to the needs of that baby. It happens with babies even under normal circumstances.

In my high school orchestra, I played second violin and loved it—at first. I felt happy to be accepted at all. Then I got to eyeing those ahead of me in the second violin section. I took extra lessons, practiced several hours a day to improve, and moved up to first chair of the second violins. But I still played only an accompaniment to the first violins.

Opposite me sat the first chair violinist of the orchestra. He was a handsome and captivating Italian boy, with music flowing through his soul and out his finger tips. His violin sang out above the whole orchestra. We all foresaw a great musical career for him. I envied him for his natural talent and his years of study. By and by he had the decency to graduate; everybody moved up and I got to play first violin. Eventually, I moved up to the second chair but never to first place. I had to conclude I would never become a remarkable violinist. The violin rested in my attic for many years until I gave it away to someone who wanted to play it.

How old was Miriam when she started playing second violin to Moses? Commentators guess she was between 7 and 15 years of age. But since girls married at 13 or 14 in those days, I believe she was probably 10 or 11. And she was certainly a very responsible child, showing poise, self-possession, cleverness, and resourcefulness.

As the baby's cries grew stronger, Jochebed knew she had to act. "And when she could no longer hide him, she took for him an ark of bulrushes, and daubed it with slime and with pitch, and put the child therein; and she laid it in the flags by the river's brink" (Ex. 2:3, KJV).

The word for "ark" is of Egyptian origin, and is used only for the arks of Moses and Noah. In both cases the ark preserved God's chosen one or ones from death by drowning. This little ark was made of bulrushes, the papyrus plant which grew along the Nile and in all its backwaters. The bulrush has a triangular stem and reaches a height of 10 to 15 feet. Ancient Egyptians used it for boat-building, for furniture, for many different purposes. Its pith supplied the ancient world with the forerunner of paper. The bulrush no longer grows wild in the lower Nile, but the Papyrus Institute in Cairo grows bulrushes in the Nile River and has revived the art of making them into papyrus.

Jochebed made the little ark watertight with slime and pitch or asphalt. Little did she know how much the infant in that ark would affect the world's history—more than any other person except Christ. She laid the box carefully among the bulrush flags at the river's brink, so it wouldn't drift downstream. Perhaps she knew the princess might come to that spot to bathe.

The Nile is a muddy river, not very inviting to bathe in. But it was considered sacred. In early times people believed the god of the Nile would grant health and fruitfulness to those who bathed in its waters. When the princess saw the strange object floating among the flags, she sent her maid to bring it to her. Perhaps she heard the tiny cries. "When she opened it, she saw the child, and behold, the boy was crying. And she had pity on him" (Ex. 2:6).

Miriam stood "at a distance" to see what would happen to the baby (Ex. 2:4). The ark left to its course would have merely postponed the tragedy. The princess left to her inclinations would have preserved the child at the expense of his nationality. Through Miriam, the two came together so that Moses' life and his nationality were both preserved.

Think of the courage it took for Miriam to approach the great princess, the daughter of a hostile king. A vast chasm of position and race separated the daughter of Pharaoh from the daughter of a slave race. Little Miriam managed to wander by quickly enough, but not too quickly. She had the wisdom and finesse to say enough but not too much. She couldn't let on that she was the baby's sister, or that she and her mother had a scheme.

The princess at once concluded, "This is one of the Hebrews' children" (Ex. 2:6). She knew about the decree. But we all know that hearing about 100,000 people devastated by an earthquake doesn't affect us nearly so much as the story of one person who is suffering.

And think of the mother's timing. A three-month-old baby has a very special appeal. Although tiny and helpless, it can smile and respond. When the princess saw a beautiful baby doomed to die, she reacted as any woman would—she wanted to save it.

Before the princess even thought through the problems of taking the child into the palace, Miriam suggested a solution. "Shall I go and call a nurse for you from the Hebrew women, that she may nurse the child for you?" (Ex. 2:7) It sounded logical—a Hebrew nurse for a Hebrew baby. The princess knew they'd need a wet nurse. And the Hebrew women who had lost their babies would have milk to give.

Pharaoh's daughter said, "Go."

Miriam, of course, called her mother. When Jochebed came, the princess gave instructions to nurse the baby for wages. Israel's future deliverer was again safe in his own home, protected by the mighty princess.

When the baby no longer needed to be nursed, Jochebed kept to her bargain. Handing her child over to the princess, she trusted

God that her own influence would remain strong enough to keep him true to the ideals of his ancestors.

Miriam Singing

Eighty years passed in the lives of Moses, Aaron, and Miriam. Moses spent 40 of these in the palace, with all its privileges and opportunities. When he sought to identify with his own Hebrew people, he accidentally killed a man and had to flee Egypt. Then he spent 40 years in the wilderness, where he learned all the wisdom of the desert. There he found a wife and fathered two sons.

When Moses was fully matured and ripened for the task, God called him back to Egypt to lead His people out. God overruled all Moses' objections to being the leader and promised him Aaron's help as spokesman.

Miriam too had developed special gifts. Later, in reviewing the Exodus, God said to Israel, "I brought you up from the land of Egypt and ransomed you from the house of slavery, and I sent before you Moses, Aaron, and Miriam" (Micah 6:4). Moses and Aaron as God's agents defeated the mighty Pharaoh. Miriam stayed in the background. At last the host of Israel left Egypt, even urged on by the Egyptians.

We now see Miriam by another body of water—this time, not the Nile River, but the Red Sea. God had given Israel a miraculous escape. "The Lord swept the sea back by a strong east wind all night, and turned the sea into dry land, so the waters were divided" (Ex. 14:21). The Egyptians were pursuing the Israelites, to bring them back as slaves. God let the water come together again, and the Egyptians were drowned.

When the children of Israel saw the Egyptians dead upon the seashore, they marveled at God's power to save. "Then Moses and the sons of Israel sang this song to the Lord" (Ex. 15:1).

All Israel entered into Moses' song, rehearsing the miracle they had seen. The song sets a pattern for later Hebrew psalms. It not only rejoices in God's accomplished acts; it rejoices in what those acts promise for the future.

Miriam, intensely attuned to Moses, rose to the moment. She led the women in a chorus of response: "Miriam the prophe., Aaron's sister, took the timbrel in her hand, and all the women went out after her with timbrels and with dancing" (Ex. 15:20).

We learn here that Miriam was a prophetess—the first woman so designated in the Bible. Others followed—Deborah (Jud. 4:4), Huldah (2 Kings 22:14), Anna (Luke 2:36). But Miriam came first.

She was the first woman in the Bible to rise to greatness entirely outside the domestic scene. We see Miriam neither in courtship nor in marriage. In a day when a single woman had little place in society, Miriam stood forth as a national figure, along with Aaron. Being a *prophetess* meant that she received special messages from God, and then gave them to the people.

She was also a leader and the first woman singer. "And Miriam answered them, 'Sing to the Lord, for He is highly exalted; the horse and his rider He has hurled into the sea'" (Ex. 15:21).

Many women are aware of God-given gifts. Says Aileen the nurse, "I know God has miraculously given me a special gift for working with sick people. A gift is to be used. I've always loved nursing.

"As I look at someone on the level above me in nursing, I'm always thinking, if I were in that position, I would certainly do things differently. I'd handle the students differently, or I'd handle the patient differently. I'm always imagining how much better my methods would have worked out, how much more the students would learn, how much sooner the patient would get well. In my fantasizing, I'm always totally successful. The patient always totally regains his faculties. Actually, all this thinking about the next step has kept me reading and striving for that next academic degree. It has kept me alert to learning new techniques."

As Miriam watched her younger brother with his great gift and commission for leadership, she didn't seem to mind playing second violin. Israel had escaped and a great future lay before them. She and her brothers formed a triumvirate, each making a distinct contribution to the national good.

Many people don't admit to suffering any feelings of envy or jealousy. I asked Priscilla, another nurse, if she ever envied the doctor. "Envy? No. I really can't say that I ever have. Sometimes I old, too professional; he doesn't have ... I never wanted to be the doctor. I have ... Each person has his own role. My role is ... necessary as his."

... hand, a young nurse whose father was an ... found nursing very frustrating. She hated always ... rs. She resented the fact that a doctor could say, "This pa... as endometriosis," while she could only say, "The patient complains of abdominal pains." A doctor could make a diagnosis and follow through with therapy. Her responsibility stopped at reporting symptoms. Jealousy led her to go to medical school and become a doctor herself.

However, not everyone wants a position of leadership and responsibility. In an office made up of six stenographers, the place of office manager became vacant. All the women were very good workers. Various ones were asked if they wanted to assume the position of manager. They didn't. One said, "I can't stand the responsibility. I'm most content when I'm doing routine work."

As parts of the body of Christ, we are complementary, each one needed, each one different (1 Cor. 12; Rom. 12; Eph. 4). No one ranks as superior or inferior in God's sight. As we learn to accept our limitations and develop our abilities, we find God's place for us.

Miriam Envying

Miriam experienced some trouble in accepting the position God marked out for her. Hers was a lofty place but Moses came first, for he carried the responsibility.

Israel had spent a year at the foot of Mount Sinai, while Moses received and delivered the Law, and instructions for the tabernacle. During that time, Aaron got mixed up in the calf worship while Moses was on the mountain. Though Aaron possessed the gift of polished speech (Ex. 4:16), his soul lacked the spiritual dimensions Moses had. He easily lost sight of the objective of their whole escape from Egypt. He listened to what people wanted to do, then did it. That's not God's idea of leadership.

We saw Miriam first by the River Nile, watching over Moses. Then we saw her by the Red Sea, joining with Moses in a great song of victory. Now we see her in the heart of the wilderness, amid vast stretches of sand and rocks, joining with Aaron in rebellion against Moses. Perhaps she grew tired of playing accompanying notes to the lead melody of her younger brother. For this time she led in jealousy and bitterness, not in exultation. "Then Miriam and Aaron spoke against Moses because of the Cushite woman whom he had married (for he had married a Cushite woman)" (Num. 12:1).

The word *Cush* refers geographically to the region south of Egypt, a land of black people. Scholars debate whether the Cushites could have included the Midianites, the people of Moses' first wife Zipporah. They also debate whether Zipporah had died, or if Moses was taking another wife in addition to Zipporah. We don't know. All we know is that Miriam disapproved of her sister-in-law.

Numbers 12:1 seems to refer to a woman he had recently married. Perhaps Miriam felt Moses was weakening his national leadership by taking a foreigner as a wife. Yet the woman may have been thoroughly suitable. Perhaps she was one of those who came out of Egypt along with the Israelites. The only foreigners God forbade marriage to were the Canaanites, those who dwelt in the land to which He was leading Israel (Ex. 34:1-16).

We know the objection came primarily from Miriam, because the verb in Numbers 12:1 is feminine: "Miriam and Aaron, she spoke." Also, her name comes first and we know already that Aaron was easily led.

Perhaps Miriam feared that Moses' wife's influence would lessen her own. Or perhaps she simply used the issue of his foreign wife as an excuse. Maybe envy of Moses had been boiling within her for some time.

We can't expect to keep feelings bottled up indefinitely. However much we intend to hide feelings we're ashamed of, we can't. Sooner or later something will happen to cause an eruption. Out will come the ugly feelings, exploding like an overheated pressure cooker hurling its contents all over the room. If we don't want ugly feelings coming out into the open, we must ask God to help us deal with them while they're still inside.

Jan felt bitterly jealous of Darlene, a fellow editorial assistant. They had a kind and generous boss, and both vied for the boss's attentions. If the boss asked the two to go out to lunch with her, Jan would refuse to go along. She wanted lunch with the boss only if she alone were invited.

Month after month Jan's growing jealousy ravaged her. She prayed about her feelings. The evening before Darlene's birthday, the Lord seemed to say very clearly to Jan, "Do something nice for Darlene on her birthday."

Jan decided to bake her a coffee cake. Said Jan, "Never in all my life did I ever bake anything with so much resentment. The next morning I didn't want to see Darlene's face when I presented the coffee cake to her. So I watched for a moment when she was away from her desk and left the cake for her.

"Darlene was overwhelmed with the gift. A week later she asked me to go to lunch with her. We walked a long way together. During that walk, my resentment melted away. Darlene and I became good friends. I've long since left that office, but today I'm better friends with Darlene than either of us is with our former boss."

Pat, a teacher in junior college, says the way to overcome jealousy is to put yourself in the other person's place. After she lost two job opportunities to black women, she put herself in their shoes, and decided she wanted them to have the jobs.

If Miriam had put herself in Moses' shoes, she would have remembered all he had to put up with. The people complained for water, they complained when they thought Moses stayed too long on the mountain, they complained about the manna. They wept and complained for the fish they ate free in Egypt, for the melons, leeks, onions, and garlic (Num. 11:1, 4-6). She would have remembered how Moses had complained to God that he couldn't carry the awful burden of all those people.

Miriam would have realized that Moses didn't need more complaints from his own brother and sister (Matt. 10:36). But she didn't put herself in Moses' shoes. She thought about how it felt in her own shoes—playing second violin to the mighty leader—her baby brother. And finally she and Aaron spoke out: "Has the Lord indeed spoken only through Moses? Has He not spoken through us as well?" (Num. 12:2)

Poor Moses. It must have seemed like the last straw. Of himself he wrote, "Now the man Moses was very humble, more than any man who was on the face of the earth" (Num. 12:3). Do you think he was bragging? I don't. I think he was only describing how he felt at the time. I think Miriam's criticism completely flattened him. He had not a word to say to her in self-defense. He hadn't wanted to take on the responsibility in the first place, and had asked God several times to relieve him of leadership. He even wanted to die to get out from under the load. Some of our greatest leaders haven't sought leadership; the responsibility sought them. They see leadership not in terms of honors and privileges, but in terms of duties and burdens.

God says we never need to defend ourselves. He promises, "Blessed are the gentle, for they shall inherit the earth" (Matt. 5:5), and "Vengeance is mine, I will repay" (Rom. 12:19).

When Moses said absolutely nothing in his own defense, God took up his cause. "And suddenly the Lord said to Moses and Aaron and to Miriam, 'You three come out to the tent of meeting.' So the three of them came out" (Num. 12:4).

God didn't waste any time in summoning the three to judgment. His speed of action suggests the importance of the issue. We are not to go through life voicing criticisms of God's appointed servants. We can pray about their faults, perhaps work together with them in overcoming weaknesses. But we're not to undermine their leadership.

"Then the Lord came down in a pillar of cloud and stood at the doorway of the tent, and He called Aaron and Miriam" (Num. 12:5). God made it very clear to Miriam and Aaron that He does the appointing. He had appointed Aaron as high priest and Miriam to the high position of prophetess, in which she would receive truth in visions and dreams. But Moses was on a different plane, for God spoke to Moses face to face, in a very special relationship. God said Miriam should have been afraid to speak against God's anointed one (Num. 12:6-8).

It's a lesson that echoes down through the ages. If God is using a servant of His through messages from the pulpit, through special ministry of various kinds, we'd better talk to God, not attack the messenger. We're not to criticize personal foibles and peculiarities of one whom God has appointed for a special task. We're to love him, support him, help him, and pray for him. We can safely leave his faults in God's hands. God will judge him as necessary.

In the case of Miriam, Aaron, and Moses, it turned out God judged Miriam as the one in the wrong. "But when the cloud had withdrawn from over the tent, behold, Miriam was leprous, as white as snow. As Aaron turned toward Miriam, behold, she was leprous" (Num. 12:10). When the cloud of God's presence departed, Miriam found herself afflicted with the most dreaded disease of that time—leprosy. The stain of her psyche—jealousy—had become outward and physical.

Aaron, like many weak people, was a person of warm affections. He loved Miriam, was horrified to see what had happened to her. He turned immediately to Moses and asked forgiveness for their presumption. "Oh, my lord, I beg you, do not account this sin to us, in which we have acted foolishly and in which we have sinned. Oh do not let her be like one dead" (Num. 12:11-12).

Responding beyond what might have been expected from one so recently wronged, "Moses cried out to the Lord, saying, 'O God, Heal her I pray!'" (Num. 12:13) Moses demonstrated his meekness, his tenderness, his care. He not only wanted his sister healed, but he wanted her healed instantly.

But the Lord said Miriam needed time to think things over. Jealousy is no light offense. He had already told Moses on the mountain, "You shall not covet . . . anything that belongs to your neighbor" (Ex. 20:17). Miriam was not to covet Moses' gifts, his special relationship with God, or his position. We each have our own very special relationship with God. We're not to covet the opportunities or responsibilities He grants to someone else.

"But the Lord said to Moses, 'If her father had but spit in her face, would she not bear her shame for seven days? Let her be shut up for seven days outside the camp, and afterward she may be received again'" (Num. 12:14). If someone who was in a position to rebuke her publicly—her father—had so rebuked her, she would have deserved seven days of being alone to think over her shortcomings. God said that the ordinary rules for leprosy would apply to Miriam (Lev. 13—14). She would go outside the camp, like any other leper, and wait seven days before presenting herself to the priest for examination and cleansing. Then, and only then, could she be received back. She needed temporary disgrace. Think of Miriam's humiliation that for a week she couldn't be touched without imparting moral uncleanness.

"So Miriam was shut up outside the camp for seven days, and the people did not move on until Miriam was received again" (Num. 12:15). Miriam, so zealous for Israel's progress, so eager to move on to the Promised Land, caused the whole camp to be delayed for seven days.

We can imagine the pall over the camp as Miriam waited for reinstatement. God must have felt they all needed to learn the lesson He was teaching to Miriam: not to criticize God's anointed. You only interfere with the progress of the whole camp by doing so.

Many a church has been stopped dead spiritually because a faction decided it didn't like the minister. Sometimes an individual says, "But the church should be more democratic. The minister shouldn't have so much to say about the direction it's to take. Hasn't God spoken by us too?" True, He has. But someone has to assume leadership. The person wanting more democracy really doesn't want other people to have their say. He, like Miriam, wants things run his way, with the minister catering to his whims. God says, "I do the appointing." Each of us is responsible to accept the position God has given to us, be it first or next to last in power.

How do you handle jealousy? A college professor says, "I handle jealousy by revising my dreams every five years or so. Your body changes as you grow older, and so do your dreams. You need to adjust your dreams to reality. Old dreams need to be given up for new ones. If you hang onto old dreams, they almost never come true. I look at my life and think, I guess I can handle that dream in the next five years, and then I work toward it. To overcome jealousy, compare yourself to people below you, not to those above. Be thankful for all God has given you."

Maybe that's the clue. "In everything give thanks; for this is God's will for you in Christ Jesus" (1 Thes. 5:18). Thank God for the gifts and opportunities He has given you. Give up the things He doesn't want you to have.

Learn from your bad experiences. Apparently Miriam did. No doubt her heart was touched and changed by her brother's love. She resumed her position of leadership and lived until just before Israel entered the Promised Land (Num. 20:1). Israelites held her in such high esteem that a form of her name, Mary, was given to many Jewish girls, including the mother of Jesus.

12
How to Succeed
in a Changed Position

Sonia was born in Minsk, Russia, a few years after the Communist revolution. She got out of Russia as a girl of 17 or 18 during World War II. "I was living in Kiev with my mother, a teacher, and my younger brother. When the Germans invaded Russia, they gathered up all the young people and took us to Stalingrad as laborers. I helped in the kitchen, peeling potatoes, washing dishes. The man I worked for was very nice. He said he had a daughter like me at home; he wouldn't let the soldiers do anything to me.

"As the Russians advanced, the Germans had to keep moving back. Often we'd pack up and move in the night. They put me in a displaced persons' camp in Poland; there again I worked for Germans. By that time I could speak German pretty well, and became a telephone operator.

"When the Russian army surrounded the Germans in Poland, thousands of Germans crowded onto a single train and went back to Germany. They took me with them."

A young Israelite maid was also torn from her country, her family, her culture. She was taken to work for foreigners. As a servant, she saw a need and suggested a remedy. In so doing she became the channel for one of the greatest miracles of the Old Testament. We learn from her the power that one person can exert. As servant in a foreign household, she brought about great results through a way of life, a set of attitudes, and a single remark.

The whole story shows that even the enemies of Israel were not beyond God's love and care.

"Now the Syrians had gone out in bands, and had taken captive a little girl from the land of Israel; and she waited on Naaman's wife" (2 Kings 5:2). When Israel proved weak, enemy countries raided her borders. Small military bands made surprise forays into the country, seized what plunder they could, killed, and carried off captives.

From time to time God uproots His people. Sometimes He puts them in difficult places, for His purposes. He put Joseph in Egypt, ultimately to provide for his whole family and nation. He put Daniel in Babylon to witness to a king and a nation. He put Paul in prison in Rome, so that the things which happened to him might further the Gospel (Phil. 1:12).

From the little maid, we can learn some hints on how to cope when life caves in, how to accept a changed position, how to make the most of a new environment. God wants something special of us in each place where He puts us.

When Life Caves In

The little maid must have nearly perished from panic when rough soldiers tore her from her home and country and bundled her off to a strange land. In that day captives meant wealth in the slave market.

A woman or girl, especially an attractive one, was valued for obvious reasons. She was also regarded as a working asset. Joseph had been sold into Egypt, and there selected as a slave for Potiphar's house. Daniel had been captured in Israel, taken to Babylon, and selected for his looks and intelligence to serve the king. The little maid must have been bright and attractive, qualified to serve as personal maid to the wife of the great captain of Syria's army.

Today we are very aware of refugees. Multitudes of people have been torn from their backgrounds. A Vietnamese family that our church is sponsoring was on a boat that was turned away from Malaysia. A younger brother, detained by the Communists, got into a separate boat which was attacked by pirates. The family saw him drown. The father and four other children finally arrived in the United States. The older brother, who had attended college in Vietnam, gratefully accepted a job doing unskilled labor.

In times of unemployment, people find themselves severed from companies they have served for many years. They accept jobs at a lower level than they have been used to. Many wives whose husbands are transferred face the difficulties of building their lives again in a new community, or sometimes in a new country.

The slave girl "waited on Naaman's wife" (2 Kings 5:2b). Who was Naaman? He's vividly sketched for us in a very few words: "Now Naaman, captain of the army of the king of Syria, was a great man with his master, and highly respected, because by him the Lord had given victory to Syria. The man was also a valiant warrior, but he was a leper" (2 Kings 5:1).

The little girl found herself not only in enemy territory, but in the very home of the man in charge of conquest! No doubt she lived happily in Israel as a daughter in her home. Now she found herself a slave. She certainly owed her new master little personal gratitude, however great he appeared to the eyes of his own people. He stood next to the king, revered as a military general who had brought deliverance to his country. Since we are told that *God* had given Naaman his great victory, we must conclude that God arranged the situation in which the girl found herself.

The little maid faced a choice. She could focus her resentment on Naaman, feed her bitterness with ugly thoughts, and dream up ways of poisoning her master. Or she could see him as a person and pity him.

Many people who cross our paths have wronged us. We face the same choice as the little maid. We can hate, resent, and steep ourselves in bitterness. Or we can see them as people created in the image of God, grieving the heart of God if they fall short of His intention.

Sonia told me of so many terrible experiences during World War II, of being separated from her family, of marrying a man in the displaced-persons camp and never seeing him again, of fleeing with her baby over the mountains at night. Physically ill, she was shifted here and there and subjected to unbelievable hardships.

And yet she always found kind people who invited her into their homes, shared with her, and took care of her for months on end.

All those tales of help she received amazed me. I asked Sonia if she thought there was anything about her personality that invited so many kindnesses.

"Well, I've always been outgoing," she said. "I love people. I think the big gift the Lord has given me is this feeling of doing things for other people. Often I take food to sick people. I'm always the one who gets up a collection to take care of some need. I like to help people and I can see what needs to be done.

"Whatever the situation, I've always tried to be friendly, to do well what was needed. When among the Germans, I saw I needed to learn the German language, and so I did. And now of course I've learned English.

"In any situation, I always see the other person's need. And for me, seeing the need is enough. I go ahead and do whatever needs doing, regardless of whether I feel like it or not. Afterward come the beautiful feelings. Afterward I get the blessing from having done what needed to be done.

"I've always been able to accept and love other people, even when they're quite different from me. Today, I have no material needs—everything is provided for. And I have my husband and family. But I still want to do as much as I can for other people because the Lord pulled me through so many hard experiences. Each day, I want Him to say to me, 'Well done.' I only hope Christ shines through me."

Naaman, whose name means "pleasant," is a picture of the natural man, enjoying the highest and best this life affords. But it all meant nothing because he had a terrible disease that was insidious, painful, loathsome, corrupting, progressive, and fatal. In Scripture, leprosy is used as a picture of sin. We know of people like Naaman who are the lions of the hour. Yet if they don't know Christ they have the equivalent of leprosy. Their successes will end in death.

If Naaman had lived in Israel, he would have been subject to the laws of quarantine, for the protection of other people. In the centuries following Bible times, millions of people died of leprosy. It was feared more than all other diseases put together. Physicians came up with wild ideas as to its causes, but their suggestions for prevention proved utterly worthless. Finally, during the Middle Ages, the church took over, and applied principles of contagion, as set forth in the Old Testament. (See Lev. 13 and 14.) At last the dread disease was brought under control. When the same principles were used during the terrible plague of the 14th century, the Black Death, it yielded its terrible grip on medieval Europe.

Thousands of years before anyone understood the germ theory of disease, the law which God gave to Israel said a leper had to live outside the camp, dress himself in a certain way, and warn others off with the cry "Unclean! Unclean!" (Lev. 13:45) It might be helpful in our society if sin were labeled contagious as leprosy was! Instead, so many things—drugs, promiscuous sex, lying, cheating—are accepted in their initial stages. Their end isn't seen.

In Syria, Naaman was accepted as a pleasant person, which no doubt he was. Because his disease was in its early stages, he could move freely in the highest society.

But he knew he was a leper. One of the greatest discoveries any of us can make is to discover that figuratively we are all lepers. We need Someone to make us clean.

Accept Change

We all want to hang onto certain things of the past. A young wife said to her husband, "I'd really like to be back having my parents take care of me."

Said the young husband, "To tell you the truth, I would too."

It isn't always easy to accept change—even to grow up. It's more comfortable to let someone else carry the load. The little Hebrew maid moved into her new responsibilities.

She did her job well. She is remembered for her witnessing to the power of the God of Israel. But no amount of witnessing at work will make up for cheating on the job. Naaman wouldn't even have listened to her if she hadn't worked industriously.

Says an architect, "I have many opportunities in my work to witness for Christ, but I confine my remarks during working hours to a sentence or two. I don't want my partners to feel that I'm using my time in the office, or taking the time of our employees, to talk about Christ."

The little girl demonstrated respect for the tasks she had to do. Today, along with the movement for women to work outside the home, I'm seeing a countermovement in the growing attitude of respect for doing housework as a living. Some women who earn money in other ways will pay a high price for household help. They recognize the ability to do housework well as a special gift.

Says Sharon, a smart young matron, "I worked in real estate for a while, and was successful, but when the market went bad, I agreed to do housework one day a week for a friend. That soon mushroomed into working every day. So I phased out of real estate. I know I'm good at housework, and that some very well-educated people aren't. The people I work for really appreciate the quality of my work.

"I like the feeling that I'm really helping people, I'm doing something needed. Some need me because of their physical disabilities, some because of limitations of time. In most of the places, I'm alone while I work. My mind is free while I work with my hands. I can listen to tapes, think about what I'm doing with my life, where my family is going, where the Lord is leading me. I've really grown spiritually because of the freedom of mind I have while doing housework."

Linda, another attractive young matron who attends one of my Bible classes, helps me at home one day a week. Says Linda, "I really love doing housework. I worked in a hospital kitchen, following diet instructions for patients' trays. But they always wanted to promote me to dietician's aid. I didn't want the responsibility. Then I worked in a discount store. I wanted to be just a little salesperson, but they always wanted to promote me. They put me in charge of sending back damaged merchandise, and I had nightmares over that job. One time a $400 television set got lost. I didn't want all those headaches. I wanted to just stay a little person.

"I found housework was really easy, discovered I could handle it, and that I loved doing it. And I feel that the families I work for really appreciate and need me. At the hospital my supervisor was constantly telling us, 'You're easily replaceable.' I guess that was her way of trying to get more work out of us. At the store too, the individual didn't count for anything. Employees were constantly coming and going.

"But in housework I'm not just another little person. I'm like an invisible member of your family—I work when you're not here. The work gives me such a peaceful feeling. When I dust your Bibles and books, I think about what you two are doing, and I'm happy to be a part of it.

"In doing housework I have more freedom and flexibility than I had in my other jobs. I never before felt proud of what I was doing, or had any sense of satisfaction about my work. Doctors and lawyers are doing work they love, and now so am I. It took me a long time to realize that my job is just as important as anyone else's. Now I can stand up to people and tell them what I do, and that I truly enjoy it. Housework doesn't seem like work to me. I like to make a window sparkle. I realize that God has given me all my energy. He's also given me a gift for doing housework well.

"Using my gift makes it possible for the doctor whose wife died recently and for my minister and his wife to use their gifts. I really feel needed."

Likewise, Naaman's wife seemed to take more than an economic interest in the Israelite maiden. She created an atmosphere where the girl felt free to express her concern for Naaman's leprosy.

Reach Out to Other People's Needs

The little maid accepted her changed situation, and did her job well. She also maintained her faith under very trying conditions. Her faith enabled her to rise above circumstances, to think in terms of another person's need, not just her own. "And she said to her mistress, 'I wish that my master were with the prophet who is in Samaria! Then he would cure him of his leprosy'" (2 Kings 5:3).

The girl maintained her faith away from home. Not everyone does. Some people leave their faith behind like unneeded clothes left in the closet. Others discard faith as they might a childhood toy. Some don't wear their faith to work, thinking it belongs with their Sunday clothes. Still others leave it behind when they go out socially. But the little maid kept her faith in God with her always, like a precious jewel, close and intimate. Like something too valuable to risk being parted from.

It wouldn't have been easy to hold onto faith in that environment. She lived in a foreign country, where they worshiped strange gods. She could have felt bitter toward God for allowing such a thing to happen to her. She could have felt so alone in her faith that she would simply slide into the idolatry she saw all around her. Instead, she maintained her own integrity. She also thought about what God could do if her new master and the great prophet in Israel could be brought together. She thought crea--tively.

She knew the miracles Elisha had performed. She had faith that God could meet the need of the great general. She merely expressed a wish. Certainly no one, least of all herself, would presume to tell the mighty Naaman how to get over his disease. But she cared about his welfare. No doubt he had already tried all possible cures of the day.

Naaman and his wife must have sensed her caring. And sensed also an authority in her faith. "And Naaman went in and told his master, saying, 'Thus and thus spoke the girl who is from the land of Israel'" (2 Kings 5:4).

How did the little maid create such a relationship with the great Naaman that he respected her suggestion?

Karen, a young minister's wife with three years of college, worked in a business office for a while. "I got out of business because I wanted to give more to my husband's ministry. And yet I find that ministry very draining.

"So I went into housework in order to free myself. My mind now feels as if I'm exercising it more than when I worked in the business office. I listen to tapes on the job; I think and I pray.

Business takes nervous energy while housework only physical energy. I wouldn't say I have a lot of energy, but I find housework a source of relaxation. Actually, I find myself getting physically stronger through doing it.

"And I'm learning so much spiritually. I find parallels to the Christian life, lessons to learn from being a servant. Christ called Himself a Servant. I have chosen to serve anybody who needs me. This is my choice—being a servant. I take pride in constantly trying to do a better job. I am willing to be a servant to anybody—I haven't yet picked different ones as better or worse to work for. Paul says we're not to think of ourselves more highly than we ought to think (Rom. 12:3). I used to find it hard to be humble, but now I know I'm elevating Him as I humble myself.

"Housework comes easy to me. I like to see things cleaned up. My mother trained me to always leave a place better than I found it—even a public restroom. In housework I'm learning a lesson essential to all relationships—to elevate the other person. Instead of thinking of my needs, I'm learning to relate to another person's needs. I'm not degrading myself in so doing. I'm simply learning to understand other people better. This helps my ministry. It also helps me in praying, for I can't really pray until I understand another's needs.

"Doing housework professionally is teaching me to discipline my mind more effectively. Since I have a certain number of hours to spend, I must schedule my tasks, do the most vital things, and keep the total job in mind. This helps me in everything I do, even in preparing for the prayer seminar I led this week."

Servanthood stands central in the Christian faith. A young man who is very successful as administrative pastor in a large church in Florida said, "I think of myself not as boss, but as servant to the staff members. I meet with each person once a week to learn how I can enable him to better fulfill his ministry in the church."

Jesus said that Gentiles like to exercise lordship and authority over other people, but it's to be different among Christ's followers. "But it is not so among you, but whoever wishes to become great among you shall be your servant; and whoever wishes to be first among you shall be slave of all. For even the Son of Man did not come to be served, but to serve, and to give His life a ransom for many" (Mark 10:43-45).

Whatever spot the Lord has put us into, the best way to fulfill our ministries is to think of ourselves as servants. We can learn from the little maidservant.

Results

The maidservant did her job well. She didn't forget her faith. And she concerned herself about her employer on a personal level. Result: the great Naaman went to Israel, was directed to Elisha, and learned the great lesson of humility himself.

Naaman drove up to Elisha's simple dwelling with his handsome entourage of horses and chariots, and waited for Elisha to come out. Instead, Elisha sent out word by a servant, "Go and take a bath. In fact, take seven baths in the River Jordan." No doubt the whole town of Samaria was watching.

Naaman found the episode humiliating to the nth degree. Everybody knew that the Jordan was a muddy river. Did Elisha think the great man Naaman was dirty? Dirtier than the River Jordan? Naaman nearly went home in a fury. But his servants persuaded him to do as the prophet had said, and he was healed.

Naaman had to learn humility. And each of us must humble himself and come to God in God's way—through faith in Christ, the living Word of God. The least is greatest, the greatest is least in the kingdom of heaven.

Elisha, faithful servant of Jehovah, refused to pander to the vanity of one the world called great. He let Naaman know he could be healed—if he took the road of humble obedience to God's plan for healing.

Fortunately, Naaman took it. He listened to his servants who advised him to do as the prophet had said. Naaman was smart enough to learn from people whom he might have viewed as inferiors. He accepted the suggestion of the servant girl. He listened to his attendants. He accepted God's plan. And he was healed.